A Healing Journey

How To Heal Grief & Rebuild Your Life After Loss

By Jennifer Farmer

Copyright © 2021 by Jennifer Farmer All rights reserved.

Ebook Adobe PDF ISBN 978-1-7351116-0-5
Paperback ISBN: 978-1-7351116-5-0

Cover and Interior Design: Kim Slater
Editors: Bessie Gantt and Trisha Kirby

Copyright
All rights reserved. Except for a single copy made for personal use only, no part of this publication may be reproduced, scanned, posted, modified, uploaded, printed, distributed, or transmitted in any form or by any means, including photocopying, recording, or other electronic or mechanical methods, without the prior written permission of the publisher, except in the case of brief quotations embodied in reviews and certain other non-commercial uses permitted by copyright law.

The author of this publication does not dispense medical advice or prescribe any technique as a form of treatment for physical, emotional or medical problems without the advice of a physician, either directly or indirectly. The intent of the author is only to offer information of general nature to help you in your quest for emotional, physical and spiritual well-being. In the event you use any of the information in this publication for yourself, the author and the publisher assume no responsibility for your action.

Jennifer Farmer LLC
P.O. Box 821052
North Richland Hills, TX 76182
Contact: info@jenniferfarmer.com
www.jenniferfarmer.com

Dedication
And Acknowledgments

This book is dedicated to my mom and dad:

You made many sacrifices to give me a great life. Thank you for your unwavering love. I love your messages and visits from the Spirit World, keep them coming. Thank you for showing me again and again that love never dies. I love you forever.

ACKNOWLEDGMENTS

Melissa Olson: Your loyal friendship, guidance and encouragement were instrumental in bringing this book to life. Thank you.

Bob Olson: Thank you for daring me to be remarkable. I am forever grateful for you. I would not be where I am today without your recommendations and guidance. Thank you for being generous with your time and knowledge. You are amazing.

Trisha Kirby: You are an angel! Your gentle spirit was exactly what I needed to get this book finished. Thank you for helping me edit this book. I appreciate you.

Kim Slater: Thank you for standing by me and believing in our God-given gifts. I'm forever grateful for your amazing support and friendship. You are gifted by God with creativity and vision. Thank you for your insights, suggestions and research for this book. Your designs are extraordinary and bring peaceful energy to this book. Thank you for putting your heart, prayers and energy in all that you create.

Helena Downer: Thank you for believing in me and in the work for the Spirit World. Thank you for your hard work in creating the first five strategy workbook. Your contributions have been invaluable in creating this book. We have got to get that bucket list trip on the schedule.

My SOS and SGM members, clients, and followers: Thank you for your love and support in my work. Thank you for allowing me to be part of your journey. You inspire me to be the best I can be. I love your enthusiasm and dedication to healing, learning and growing. Keep serving Spirit for the greater good. Never give up.

My family and friends: Betty, Matt, James, Katee, Bubba, Patricia, Kassy, Diana, Pam, Prudence, JoEllen, Lynn, Karyn, Beth, Sherri and the many wonderful friends not mentioned. Thank you for your everlasting love and support. My life is better because you are in it. I love you always.

Thank you to my Spirit Guides, Angels and departed loved ones in the Spirit World. You have helped me heal, grow and share with others. You are the best.

God: You saved my life many years ago. Thank you for sending all your angels to help me. Thank you for the many gifts and miracles since that time. I'm so glad that I got a second chance. I know every day on this earth is a gift.

Table of Contents

How to Use This Book 07

Healing Journey Checklist 09

Chapter 1 • *Death Is Not the End* 11
    Exercise 1: Understanding Your Grief 26
    Worksheet #1 Personal Discovery Assessment 28
    Exercise 2: What is Grief Exactly? 34
    Worksheet #2 What has Changed? 35
    Worksheet #3 Personal Reflection 39

Chapter 2 • **Strategy 1** • *Giving Yourself Permission* 41
    Exercise 3: Giving Yourself Permission Example 50
    Worksheet #4 Love Letter to Yourself 51
    Worksheet #5 Personal Reflection 53

Chapter 3 • **Strategy 2** • *Plan for the Stormy Weather* 55
    Exercise 4: Preparing for Those Days 59
    Worksheet #6 Stormy Weather Plan 60
    Worksheet # 7 Personal Reflection 63

Chapter 4 • **Strategy 3** • *Rest, Repair, Rebuild* **65**
    Exercise 5: Rest, Repair, Rebuild Overview **73**
    Worksheet #8 Rest, Repair, Rebuild **74**
    Exercise 6: Forgiveness **83**
    Worksheet #9 Forgiveness **84**
    Exercise 7: Gratitude **86**
    Worksheet #10 Gratitude **87**
    Worksheet #11 Personal Reflection **89**

Chapter 5 • **Strategy 4** • *Get A New Purpose* **91**
    Exercise 8: Get a New Purpose **97**
    Worksheet #12 Your New Life Purpose **98**
    Worksheet #13 Personal Reflection **101**

Chapter 6 • **Strategy 5** • *Connect to the Spirit World* **103**
    Exercise 9: Connect to the Spirit World **122**
    Worksheet #14 Letter to the Spirit World **124**
    Exercise 10: Make the Connection with Meditation **127**
    Meditation Experience Journal **129**
    Meditation 1 *Clear Your Mind Meditation* Practice **140**
    Meditation 2 *Awareness Meditation* Practice **143**
    Meditation 3 *Healing Grief With the Spirit World Meditation* Practice **144**
    Next Steps **148**

With the purchase of this book, you receive free access to an online learning library for this book as an added bonus. This online library is accessible from your smart phone, computer or tablet. It includes: guided meditations, MP3 downloads, a place to share your insights and a .pdf version of the book for printing additional worksheets as needed. For your free bonus access, go to **https://jenniferfarmer.com/bookbonus/**

How to Use this Book

This book is offered in the Spirit of Love. I created this book and exercises to guide and support your healing journey. Healing grief takes time, energy and self-care. It does not happen overnight.

To get the most out of the book and exercises, I recommend reading a chapter and then working on the exercises for that chapter. Give yourself time to digest and put the exercises into practice. Then start the next chapter when you are ready.

Each chapter and its exercises are stepping stones that build upon each other so it's best to do them in order. If you get overwhelmed with a chapter or exercise, I encourage you to move on to the next chapter or exercise. When you are ready, return to the unfinished chapter or exercise to complete it. You have my express permission to print out the exercises in this book for your personal use only.

You don't have to do all the exercises to find relief. If you feel overwhelmed with an exercise, set it aside for a day or two and then return to it.

In writing this book, I visualized the reader reading each chapter, completing the exercises and then taking time between each chapter to apply the exercises. As you are in charge of your own journey, work at a pace that is right for you.

My recommendation is to apply the tools and suggestions in the exercises for three to six months to get the best results. This book does not offer treatment or replace any medical treatment, legal, professional or financial advice. The exercises in this book may complement other healing practices. Due to the nature and individuality of each person's healing process, results may vary for each person and results cannot be guaranteed. The reader is solely responsible for their own actions and results.

As you begin your healing journey, keep your mind open as you read each chapter and complete the exercises. Your experience and results will be unique to you. Know that you are a miracle and never give up on yourself.

Take a couple of minutes before you get started and request for your free online learning library bonus access.

https://jenniferfarmer.com/bookbonus/

The library includes: guided meditations, MP3 downloads, a place to share your insights and a .pdf version of the book for printing additional worksheets as needed.

Feel free to email me at **info@jenniferfarmer.com** if you have questions along your journey.

Jennifer Farmer

Healing Journey Checklist

Using this checklist will help you complete each step of your healing journey. Take your time as you work through the exercises. Move to the next chapter when you are ready. If you get overwhelmed with an exercise, move to the next exercise or chapter, then return to the unfinished chapter or exercise when you are ready. Remember to celebrate each step of the way.

STEP	PAGE	STARTED	COMPLETED
☐ Read Chapter 1 • **Death is not the End**	11		
☐ Read Exercise 1	26		
☐ Complete Worksheet #1 Personal Discovery Assessment	28		
☐ Read Exercise 2	34		
☐ Complete Worksheet #2 What has Changed?	35		
☐ Complete Worksheet #3 Personal Reflection	39		

Well done! You've taken a courageous step forward in your journey. Keep going.

☐ Read Chapter 2 • Strategy 1 • **Giving Yourself Permission**	41		
☐ Read Exercise 3	50		
☐ Complete Worksheet #4 Love Letter to Yourself	51		
☐ Complete Worksheet #5 Personal Reflection	53		

You are doing awesome. Do something for YOU this week to celebrate your progress.

STEP	PAGE	STARTED	COMPLETED
☐ Read Chapter 3 • Strategy 2 • **Plan for the Stormy Weather**	55		
☐ Read Exercise 4	59		
☐ Complete Worksheet #6 Stormy Weather Plan	60		
☐ Complete Worksheet #7 Personal Reflection	63		

You are making great progress. Plan a special activity to celebrate.

☐ Read Chapter 4 • Strategy 3 • **Rest, Repair, Rebuild**	65		
☐ Read Exercise 5	73		
☐ Complete Worksheet #8 Rest, Repair, Rebuild	74		
☐ Read Exercise 6	83		
☐ Complete Worksheet #9 Forgiveness	84		
☐ Read Exercise 7	86		
☐ Complete Worksheet #10 Gratitude	87		
☐ Complete Worksheet #11 Personal Reflection	89		

You've made a HUGE step in your healing journey. Schedule a fun outing.

☐ Read Chapter 5 • Strategy 4 • **Get a New Purpose**	91		
☐ Read Exercise 8	97		
☐ Complete Worksheet #12 Your New Life Purpose	98		
☐ Complete Worksheet #13 Personal Reflection	101		

Outstanding! Email Jennifer at info@jenniferfarmer.com and share your new purpose.

☐ Read Chapter 6 • Strategy 5 • **Connect to the Spirit World**	103		
☐ Read Exercise 9	122		
☐ Complete Worksheet #14 Letter to the Spirit World	124		
☐ Read Exercise 10	127		
☐ Complete 21-Day Meditation Journal	129		
☐ Take Next Steps	148		

Time for a big celebration! Do something extra special for you.

CHAPTER 1

Death
Is Not the End

When my dad passed, I wanted my life to end. I wanted to be with him. I even had a plan to go. I was so mad at everything and everyone that he died. Thankfully Divine intervention put that plan on pause.

For me to recover and heal from his death, I had to go so far beyond what I knew. I had to go deep and find something beyond myself. Connecting to the Spirit World came to my rescue in the time of my greatest need, then and now. Partnering with the Spirit World dramatically changed how I think and feel about life. I know I am not alone in this world.

I've been blessed and feel a personal obligation to God and the Spirit World to give back my knowledge and experience to help others. I feel called to serve you and others who want to grow spiritually and heal their lives with the power of the Spirit.

> *I feel called to serve you and others who want to grow spiritually and heal their life with the power of the Spirit.*

I've faced many challenges, including prolonged grief, overwhelming fear, chronic pain, my hopes and dreams burning to the ground, major financial difficulties, and personal and professional disappointments and challenges. Armed with determination, perseverance, and Divine help from God, my Spirit Guides, Angels, and my loved ones in the Spirit World, I've overcome many of these challenges and landed on my feet. I've found real moments of relief and freedom from the pain of grief, loss, and disappointment. Many of my days are now filled with peace, love, and joy.

You, my friend, can have the same experience. Recovery is possible. Living a full life is possible. The Spirit World is open to all who seek. Its universal power is love. Your Spirit Team loves you unconditionally. Your team is your Highest Self, God, Spirit Guides, Angels, Ascended Masters, and your loved ones. They bring love, healing, support, wisdom, comfort, and evidence of the Afterlife.

I'm really glad that you're here. It means a lot to me that you would allow me to help you on your journey. My goal is to walk you through your healing process toward peace, relief, and freedom from the painful emotions brought on by the loss you've experienced in your life.

The five-strategy process I'm going to share with you in this book is so important. Each strategy, each step, clears the painful energy and emotions so you can experience the amazing love and support that the Spirit World offers. The first four of the five strategies clear the way for the success of the final step, connecting to the Spirit World.

You've given yourself a great gift. You'll get a chance to reflect, rest, restore, and rebuild your life and how you perceive it. My sincere hope is that you will embrace and explore all five strategies including creating a powerful connection with the Spirit World.

The key is to have strategies to relieve and overcome fear, regret, anger, depression, and other painful emotions that cast a heavy shadow in your heart and mind.

Nobody really likes to talk about anxiety, depression, fear, loss, or grief because most people, me included, want to avoid painful emotions. Most people wish it would just go away or be gone as fast as possible. We all want to be okay. Who really wants to suffer until the bitter end?

It's completely normal to want to escape, repress, and deny the pain we feel inside. Hiding from and not addressing what's really going on is a coping mechanism for many. We live in a culture that has a pill to fix everything that ails us. The cosmetic industry tells us we can feel better on the inside if we fix the outside. Yes, these things can give you relief for a while. Sooner or later, though, our soul asks to acknowledge, honor, and express painful emotions that lie under the surface. Facing the pain is not easy. It can be really scary.

Fearful thoughts creep in that can block healing and real recovery.

Thoughts like these:
- I can't handle the pain.
- I am not sure I can survive reliving it again.
- What's the point? Nothing will change.

You were born to shine your light and love in this world—now more than ever. You can't truly shine your light and express love in this world unless you have the courage to face the painful emotions from grief. The key is to have strategies to relieve and overcome fear, regret, anger, depression, and other painful emotions that cast a heavy shadow in your heart and mind. The payoff for facing grief head-on is big. You don't have to be a victim of your own life. You can opt out of prolonged suffering.

On this journey together, we are going to tap into the power of your Higher Self. Your Higher Self, what some call your soul or spirit, has a unique calling. Your Higher Self's DNA code has everything you need to recover, heal, and fulfill your personal greatness, which is to be full of self-love and fearlessly share your love in the world without fear, worry, or regret.

First of all, when we talk about grief, it stops most of us in our tracks. We get into this holding zone where it's hard to move forward because it seems overwhelming and impossible to overcome. Worse yet, fear can paralyze us from moving forward.

Some common fears that can delay or prevent healing and relief:
- We're afraid that if we let go of the pain, we'll have nothing left to hang on to that connects us with our loved ones.
- We're afraid our loved one is going to think we forgot them or, worse yet, that we will forget them.
- We're afraid other people are going to judge how we handle our grief or the way we try to move forward.
- We're afraid we're going to make a mistake.
- We're afraid we're not going to be enough or do enough.

The truth is that living with loss is new and unfamiliar territory. New tools and skills are needed to recover and heal. If you don't pick up the tools, your heart will never reach its full capacity to love. I'm going to help you one step at a time. You can always take a break when you need to.

Keep in mind that grief enters our lives in many ways and at different times without warning. It's not only when a loved one dies. Unresolved grief from childhood can lie low under the surface of your awareness causing depression and anxiety.

Losses and trauma that you didn't or couldn't safely grieve as a child or as an adult at an earlier time in life can be an underlying source of chronic physical issues, addictions, and problems with intimacy and relationships. You are strong enough now to look at the impacts of unresolved grief. Your Higher Self led you here. This is an excellent sign. Your inner Spirit is letting you know you are safe and strong enough now. It's time to find peace, to grow and heal.

Sometimes, the repression is so deep you may not even be aware of how it has impacted your life. I'll share an example—my grandmother died when I was sixteen. A few years ago, I was doing a review of my "Healing with the Spirit World" meditation. Out of the blue, unexpectedly, my grandmother showed up while I was doing the practice. I could see her in my mind's eye. It was like she was standing right in front of me, with her rolling pin in hand. I don't exactly know how she was able to do it. She sent an all-encompassing feeling of love through my entire being. I felt true unconditional love from her for several moments. When I finished the meditation, I felt some part of my soul was healed.

You see, I loved my grandma so much. She was my guardian in many ways. I held so much regret in my soul and felt like I didn't deserve her love because I did not go see her in the nursing home as often as I thought I could have. When she came into the meditation, it was so powerful in healing my shame and regret over how that relationship ended. I was a teenager at the time and wanted to have fun. I didn't make time to spend time with her. Almost thirty years later, she showed up in the meditation and healed a part of my soul that I didn't even know needed healing.

Trauma can bring up feelings of loss and grief. Maybe you lost your innocence too early in life. Maybe you are grieving the loss of a marriage or the loss of a partner. Maybe your financial situation or health has changed and you're grieving the loss of a way of life, money, and freedom.

Maybe you had your heart set on getting married, having a big family, lots of money, a house full of kids, living in a certain place, starting your own business, or achieving some physical goal, but life gave you something else.

Maybe you're feeling stuck or you're just struggling. You still have time. You are worth it. You can create a life worth living that includes joy, love, and freedom. Loss and grief will happen in life, and even though we can't control when it happens or how it happens, we can control how we handle it. You get to choose how you recover and heal. Some losses, we don't get over—we get through them, striving, reaching, hoping to keep our heart and mind open to love and to being loved.

You are further along in your healing than you think. Wherever you are on your path, your Higher Self, the Spirit within, knows you are ready and strong enough to heal and shine your light. You are in the right space here because at some level you made a decision to heal your heart and mind. This a huge first step. The first step is always the hardest to take.

There are many methods one can use when it comes to managing and coping with grief and loss. Some good, some not so good. In an effort to heal, we try meditation and mantras. We try counseling, group therapy, support groups, going to church, praying, and medication. These are all awesome tools. I encourage you to continue to use them while working through the exercises in this workbook. But keep an eye out for any self-destructive behaviors—like isolation, shopping therapy (creating a lot of debt in the process), falling into addiction or alcoholism, getting in or staying in unhealthy or abusive relationships—to cope with pain, fear, loss, and grief.

If you are on a self-destructive path or isolating from life, I understand. I've been there too. I encourage you to seek out professional help, support groups, or 12-step recovery programs in your healing process. There is no shame or regret in self-destructive coping methods. Do your best to get help and do these behaviors less. We all do the best we can with what we know until we know and can do better.

You and I will work together with the strategies in this workbook so you can improve your self-confidence, become full of self-love, and shine your love in the world without fear, worry, or regret. How does that sound?

We've tried a lot of different things to cope with grief. Now we're going to try something else. We're going to explore five strategies and tap into the power of your Higher Self to help you get to wholeness and fulfill your spiritual greatness. You and I will work together with the strategies in this workbook so you can improve your self-confidence, become full of self-love, and shine your love in the world without fear, worry, or regret. How does that sound?

One small note, a legal disclaimer. I'm not a psychologist or professional counselor, and this book is not intended to replace professional, medical, or legal advice. My hope is that it will accelerate your healing process and complement any therapeutic methods you explore on your healing journey.

My goal is to help you navigate your healing journey on the road to find peace and to let you know that you're not alone. My teaching style is to share stories and real-life examples to help you recognize where you are and what your next steps will be.

I have experienced many losses in my life. I lived with painful regrets for years. I turned to all the wrong paths to cope with my pain, guilt, and suffering when my dad died. I had no clue how to cope or get through the pain of his death. In our family, we just pretended everything was normal. Nobody talked about real feelings or problems in our family. I was so angry at him because he basically drank himself to death. When he passed, the depression became unbearable. I wanted to die, and I had a plan for that.

The good news is God had a bigger plan for me. My dad's death taught me how to live. I've felt at times that my dad made the ultimate sacrifice so I could live and have the amazing life I have now. You see, he was my first connection to the Spirit World. When my dad died, I didn't know that I could connect with him in the Spirit World. I just thought his death was the end. I thought I would live with my guilt, anger, and regret forever, but instead his death was the catalyst that opened the door of the Spirit World to me. Connecting to the Spirit World is one of the strategies we'll cover in the book. I'll share more about that later.

Another big loss for me was my dog Sam. She was my friend and workout companion, and she helped me through a big relationship break-up. She was a great comfort to me. I know that she is definitely a part of my healing work now. Since she passed, she has helped me connect to the unconditional love of animals. From time to time, I see her out of the corner of my eye and know she is reminding me to connect with my love of animals. Animals have helped me so much in my healing journey—the ones on this side and the ones in Heaven.

My mom passed in 2017. I'm not over it completely. She will be part of my life until I see her again in Spirit. It's been a big change in my life to have both of my parents in Spirit. I know now that I can connect to the Spirit World and talk to my mom and my other loved ones in Spirit. There was a significant difference in my level of pain and how I've moved through grief knowing that they are still with me. It has brought me great comfort and healing.

I like to think of the five stages of grief as points in the journey of grief. Knowing where we are is powerful in the healing process.

Along my healing journey, I came across a book written by Elizabeth Kübler-Ross. She was a psychiatrist who dedicated much of her life's work to helping people through grief. I loved reading her work and found comfort in her books. They helped me get some clarity about death and grieving. She outlined five stages of grief: denial, anger, bargaining, depression, and acceptance. Knowing the five stages is the road map, the mile markers of grief. For myself and many of my clients and students, however, just knowing what the stages are is not enough to find lasting peace.

I like to think of the five stages of grief as points in the journey of grief. Knowing where we are is powerful in the healing process. The five stages guide us through the behaviors, feelings, and processes of grief. They are milestones that let you know that you're still alive. When you experience a loss, you go through a period of shock, even if the passing was expected. Numbness sets in and helps us cope until we are strong enough to take the next step. In shock, we say things like, *"I just can't believe I'll never see them again"* and *"I was just talking to them yesterday."* Apathy also makes an appearance, with *"What's the point?"* or *"It doesn't matter anymore."*

I'm going to share a little of my experience with the five stages to help you recognize some of the feelings of each one. I'll share a learning or insight I've gained through the experience. I still experience grief. It's not as intense and does not stay with me as long. I do my best to apply the strategies in this book to help me through them.

DENIAL

Listen, I love denial. I really do. I learned early on how useful it could be in coping with my family's problems. We looked good on the outside: nice house, nice clothes, parents working, two cars in the driveway. Inside the house, we were a dysfunctional mess.

Denial saved me from a lot of chaos in my inner and outer worlds. I know how to pretend like nothing is going on. And for me, that was a good coping skill growing up in the family I did—with my dad's drinking and how we as a family didn't address it.

Denial, escaping, and repression really can help us get through the hard times in life. I've discovered over time that our souls long for truth, acknowledgment, and to express love. It won't rest until we do. Our soul is like the sun. The sun rises and sets every day no matter what the day brings. The human soul and spirit is designed to help us rise from the ashes, to move forward, to live and love again.

When my mom died, I was in shock for weeks. I knew she died, but I found myself thinking, I better call Mom on Saturday. She'll want to hear how things are going here in Florida. I found myself saying, *"I just can't believe it."*

You may not feel like it now or think it's even possible. I'm not trying to rush you through your healing journey. You can heal and move forward at a pace that is right for you.

Please keep this in mind: if you are living and breathing, you are a miracle. Life is a gift. You have so much more living to do, more chapters to experience, more love to give and receive. Recognizing and moving through denial, escaping, and repression can help you move forward and create a new chapter of growth, healing, and recovery. I'm living proof of what is possible.

ANGER

I believe anger is a tool God gave us to protect ourselves. You may not experience anger at your lost loved one, but you may experience anger at God. Why am I going through this? Why can't it be? Why do I have to deal with all of this? Why me? You may even turn anger in on yourself, showing up as perfectionism, irritation, anxiety, or depression.

BARGAINING

I spent a lot of time in the bargaining phase with my dad before and after he died. I experienced grief for almost two years while watching him drink himself to death.

I actually lost my dad to alcohol before he died. I would beg God: *"Please, God, I promise I'll do whatever you want me to do if you help me get him sober."*

Years after his death, I replayed every detail of his death in my head, especially when I longed to see him on Father's Day and missed him on holidays, his birthday, and the anniversary date of his death. I replayed our last conversation, getting the notification telephone call, and going over to his house after his funeral over and over in my head.

- If only I had gone to see him, maybe he would not have died.
- If I hadn't told him that I couldn't see him because of his drinking, would he still be here?
- Why didn't I call him back and tell him how much I loved him?

Telling the story over and over and asking these questions again and again—does it sound like a familiar experience in your life?

Even after all this time, I experience moments of bargaining when it comes to my dad. His death took a toll on my soul. Learning to communicate with him and recognizing the messages he has given me has brought me great relief. Now I know he watches over me and other family members here. I know he is in a better place and that he knows I love him.

DEPRESSION

This has been and still is the most difficult stage in the grief process for me to recognize and acknowledge. I got really good at pretending everything was okay. A few months after he died, it hit me that my dad had died and was never coming back. Darkness settled over me. I was the walking dead. Yes, my hair and makeup looked great. I went to work and paid my bills on time, but I was just a shell. I felt like I had nothing to live for. I had no clue how to deal with the emptiness that consumed me. I lived day in and day out with despair, loneliness, regret, and guilt. I went on a six-month drinking binge, wishing for the end. The plans I made to end it all did not happen.

God sent Angels to help me find another way, and I'm forever grateful. I have not had a drink since then. I'd like to say that after that I experienced no more depression, but that would be a lie. In dealing with depression, I put all my energy into work and became a workaholic. I stayed so busy in life that I could not sit still for five minutes. If I did, it might all come back and swallow me whole.

The thing I've learned about depression is that it's a normal response to loss. If you give it space to breathe, acknowledge it, and express it, depression will pass. If you resist it or try to repress it, it will persist. I've gotten better at recognizing and honoring my feelings. I don't run from them. I write them down and share them with safe and supportive friends and family. Honoring feelings is part of the healing process.

ACCEPTANCE

Acceptance means that we've accepted the reality of the loss. We know we are in some level of acceptance when we start considering ways to move forward. I'm so glad acceptance does not require us to like the reality. I've accepted that my dad died. Knowing that he is with my mom and others brings me peace. I'm comforted to know that he is free of suffering. I know he loves me. I've accepted that my mom died. I'm happy my mom and dad are together and finally love each other fully.

Where would you say you are in all of these stages of grief?
Number one, it's not the same for everybody. Going through grief is not 1, 2, 3, it's over. It not linear. It's messy, it hurts, it goes away for a while and comes back without any warning. It shows up years later and in different life experiences. As an example, I didn't really give myself a chance to grieve the innocence I lost as a child until I was in my late thirties and early forties. As long as we are living and breathing, we will experience some level of grief in our lifetime.

You don't have to go through all the stages, but it's helpful to know where you are in the healing process—it gives you some self-awareness and can bring clarity and hope. It helps you identify and acknowledge what you are feeling. When you know where you are right now, you can assess what the next step is and how to move forward. Planning your next step is a powerful part of moving forward on your healing journey. Start where you are without judging yourself.

Have hope. I'm here to tell you that I have found a way to live with my loss. It doesn't mean that I don't experience pain and suffering from time to time. Grief shows up more around anniversaries and important dates. As I heal from other losses in my life, grief crops up when I enter into a new phase of personal and spiritual growth. The difference now is that 1) I have tools to handle loss, and 2) the level of suffering that I go through is far better than what it used to be.

As you read through this guide book and think about each exercise at the end of the chapters, I encourage you to give yourself the opportunity to really immerse yourself in the process. You may want to print out the exercises ahead of time. You can find the printable version in your learning library. You are embarking on a healing journey. It's good to prepare in advance for each reading or exercise ahead of time:

- First, find a quiet space for reading and working on the exercises. Pick a spot that makes you happy and where you feel safe.
- Give yourself time. Carve out a time when you know you will not be interrupted and you can turn off your phone. This is a valuable time to evaluate, reflect, and prioritize. Work at your own pace.
- Select your tools. Use a brightly colored pen to make the exercises fun and bring a positive energy. Have a refreshing drink on hand to keep you hydrated and comfortable.
- Finally, breathe. Take a deep breath in and out slowly. Feel yourself relax and your mind focus. Concentrate on this for one minute. Invite your Spirit Team and your Higher Self to help you with this process. Set your intention: I love and appreciate myself. I am strong. I am capable. I am ready to shine my light.

You may have moments of sadness, overwhelm, or anger come up as you are working on the exercises. Honor your feelings and give them space to breathe. I try to remember that where I am in this moment is not permanent. Grief is a living experience, a doorway into a journey, not a place to stay. Grief is not a sign of weakness or a lack of faith. Some people say it's the price of love.

Healing is a choice. It is never too late to make that choice, wherever you are in the grieving process. There are no time limits, no pressure, no judging.

In this workbook, I want to share with you the tools, the five strategies, that have helped me so that you too can start a new path toward recovery, healing, and peace. We'll discuss each strategy in depth. My suggestion is to work through the strategies in order and to take a break for a couple days if you get overwhelmed.

It does not matter how long it's been since your loss or trauma. It could be twenty year ago or last week. Trust that you were drawn to this workbook NOW because there is one small shift, a breakthrough, and moments of relief waiting for you. Love yourself enough to choose healing and take each step little by little. You may be by yourself, but you are never alone.

The exercises at the end of each chapter will help you gain clarity along the way so you discover and create the life you want. You'll create an action plan to help you achieve your goals. Here are the five strategies we'll be working on:

1. Give Yourself Permission.
2. Plan for the Weather.
3. Rest, Repair and Rebuild.
4. Get a New Purpose.
5. Connect to the Spirit World.

Imagine yourself being free of fear and worry and letting go of guilt and regret. Take a moment and think about what your life could feel like without these in your mind and heart.

Now you are ready. It takes willingness and courage to start over after loss and disappointment. We'll do it here together. Through these strategies and exercises, you will be able to take small intentional steps to rebuild and redesign your life with more peace, joy, and connection to the inexhaustible power of Spirit.

Imagine yourself being free of fear and worry and letting go of guilt and regret. Take a moment and think about what your life could feel like without these in your mind and heart. Very good. Now, imagine feeling whole and healing your sense of loss. Imagine waking up with energy and focus, finding new purpose and a deeper understanding of the Spirit you are. Visualize going about your day connecting to your loved ones, with your Spirit Guides and Angels comforting you, feeling supported, being empowered, and being connected to love. All of these are possible! Let's turn the page and start the journey.

EXERCISE 1

UNDERSTANDING YOUR GRIEF

How We Want Grief To Work

How Grief Actually Works

Experiencing loss is part of life. Coping, moving forward and healing are different for everyone. There are NO set rules or perfect way to grieve. There are NO typical responses to loss or time limits for when grieving should or will be over.

Walking through grief is deeply personal and unique.

Most importantly, it is an emotional experience not always seen by the physical eye. It lives deep in our hearts and minds. Healing the pain of grief has a lot of stops, starts, twists and turns.

To me, grief is like the weather. You can't control it; you can only go through it. Just like the weather, the emotional forecast is different every day. It changes and moves through the mind and heart. It has a life of its own. Some days, the forecast is clear and sunny. Some days it feels like a tornado or hurricane that rips through the heart and mind, leaving nothing left but the pieces to pick up and put back together. When I'm in the thick of it, I do my best to remember, *"this too shall pass."*

EXERCISE 1

The Five Stages of Grief created by Elizabeth Kubler Ross are milestones that put a name to what you are going through while learning to live again. They are guide posts to help you understand your feelings and where you are in your healing process. You may go through some or all of the stages – with no prescribed order. You may experience more time in one stage and less to no time in another.

> You don't have to experience all of the stages of grief to heal and find peace.

MILESTONES OF THE FIVE STAGES OF GRIEF

Chart Source: The Kübler-Ross model, or the five stages of grief was created by psychiatrist Elisabeth Kübler-Ross in her 1969 book On Death and Dying.

WORKSHEET 1

PERSONAL DISCOVERY ASSESSMENT

These questions will help you discover where you are in your healing process. It may bring thoughts and feelings that do not have any connection to a recent loss. Go ahead and write down whatever comes to mind. There are no right or wrong answers. This is for your self-awareness. If you don't have an answer or you get overwhelmed, you can come back to it. Take your time in answering the questions.

WHERE ARE YOU NOW? (CIRCLE)

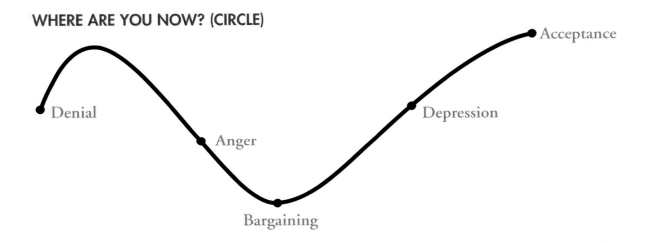

WHAT OR WHO ARE YOU GRIEVING?

_____
_____
_____
_____
_____
_____
_____

WORKSHEET 1

WHAT EXPERIENCES ARE YOU MISSING?

_____
_____
_____
_____
_____
_____
_____

WHAT IS MAKING YOU ANGRY?

_____
_____
_____
_____
_____
_____
_____

WHAT MAKES YOU SAD?

_____
_____
_____
_____
_____
_____
_____

WORKSHEET 1

WHAT IS MAKING YOU AFRAID OR ANXIOUS?
_____
_____
_____
_____
_____
_____
_____

WHAT IS MAKING YOU FEEL OVERWHELMED?
_____
_____
_____
_____
_____
_____
_____

WHAT IS MAKING YOU WANT TO "RUNAWAY OR HIDE"?
_____
_____
_____
_____
_____
_____
_____

WORKSHEET 1

WHAT IS MAKING YOU FEEL CONFUSED?

_____
_____
_____
_____
_____
_____
_____

WHAT SITUATIONS MAKE YOU THINK "IF ONLY I..."?

_____
_____
_____
_____
_____
_____
_____

WHAT IS MAKING YOU FEEL GUILTY?

_____
_____
_____
_____
_____
_____
_____

WORKSHEET 1

WHAT ACTIONS HAVE YOU TAKEN TO COPE WITH YOUR GRIEF AND LOSS?

_____
_____
_____
_____
_____
_____
_____
_____
_____
_____

WHAT WOULD YOU LIKE TO HEAL OR ACHIEVE WITH THIS GUIDE BOOK?

_____
_____
_____
_____
_____
_____
_____
_____
_____
_____

WORKSHEET 1

YOUR PERSONAL REFLECTIONS:

___

QUESTIONS FOR JENNIFER:

___

EXERCISE 2

WHAT EXACTLY IS GRIEF?

Grief is normal. *IT'S A NATURAL REACTION TO A SIGNIFICANT EMOTIONAL LOSS OF ANY KIND.* It has many emotions within it. It's a feeling of being overwhelmed, an inner pain caused by the loss of a loved one, an unexpected or expected change in life, belief pattern or behavior.

Grief can happen before an actual loss. For example:
- My mom went into a nursing home long before she passed. Her health changed overnight and she was bed ridden. I grieved the change of her life with her.
- My dad was a chronic alcoholic. I watched him drink himself to death. It was very painful to watch him lose everything to his addiction including his life. I grieved for the dad that was sober years before he died.

Unresolved grief can show up long after a loss. *THOUGHTS AND FEELINGS OF "I JUST CAN'T" ARE AT THE FOREFRONT OF THE MIND.* Grief brings up feelings of loss when you reach for someone or something that has always been there but is no longer there. A variety of life events and experiences of loss can trigger grief: Death of a loved one, dreams, goals not achieved, life not working out as expected, and past or present trauma.

> "Grief never ends, but it changes. It's a passage, not a place to stay. Grief is not a sign of weakness, not a lack of faith... it is the price of love."
> —Author Unknown

Here's the good news: YOU CAN GET THROUGH IT. Why? Because you are stronger than you think!

WORKSHEET 2

WHAT HAS CHANGED?

HOW HAVE YOU CHANGED SINCE YOUR LOSS?
Without judgment, list all positive or negative changes.

_____
_____
_____
_____
_____
_____
_____
_____
_____
_____
_____
_____
_____
_____
_____

WORKSHEET 2

WHAT IDEAS AND BELIEFS HAVE CHANGED?
Note: INCLUDE POSITIVE CHANGES TOO!

_____
_____
_____
_____
_____
_____
_____
_____
_____

WHAT HAVE YOU STOPPED DOING? HAS THIS BEEN FOR YOUR HIGHEST GOOD?

_____
_____
_____
_____
_____
_____
_____
_____
_____
_____
_____
_____
_____

WORKSHEET 2

WHO HAVE YOU STOPPED SEEING?
If this is a positive change, write it down too.

_____
_____
_____
_____
_____
_____
_____
_____
_____

WHAT HAVE YOU BEEN AFRAID TO DO?
Include fears you have faced and overcome.

_____
_____
_____
_____
_____
_____
_____
_____
_____

WORKSHEET 2

REFLECTION:

STEP 1: Go back and read through the changes you described.

STEP 2: Write down any additional things that come to mind when you read your entries.
   NOTE: No self-judgment.

STEP 3: Put a star next to any wins and progress you have made.

STEP 4: Put a check mark next to anything you would like to do differently in the future.

WHAT AREAS WOULD YOU LIKE TO CHANGE IN THE FUTURE?

_____
_____
_____
_____
_____
_____
_____
_____
_____
_____
_____
_____
_____
_____
_____
_____
_____

WORKSHEET 3

YOUR PERSONAL REFLECTIONS:

___

QUESTIONS FOR JENNIFER:

___

CHAPTER 2

Giving yourself Permission

You're exactly where you are supposed to be in this moment. Your Higher Self has led you here. You may be struggling. IT'S OKAY. There will be struggles ahead, but you have what it takes to start heal starting now. The most powerful healings and transformations start with making a small decision. We all have to start somewhere.

Happiness and joy were inconceivable to me after my dad died. I didn't know how to be happy without him here. I didn't feel like I deserved to be happy or have joy. Guilt and regret planted themselves in my mind and heart. I never told anyone how many times I wanted to drive off the bridge but just couldn't find the courage. I could function with a smile on my face. Depression does not always look like depression.

At some point, there was a shift in me. It came almost three years after my dad died. I'm not sure exactly when or where it happened. In the quiet moments while driving to and from work, I sensed that God wanted something more for me. There was an inner nudge. I was given a second chance at life for a good reason. I hoped for peace and started to believe it was possible.

Life filled with prolonged sadness, guilt, shame, anger, regret and fear is painful.

Life filled with prolonged sadness, guilt, shame, anger, regret, and fear is painful. You were not put on this earth to suffer. Being willing to let go of the need to suffer and to hold on to your pain, opens the door to peace. Easier said than done, for sure. It has taken me many years to change my beliefs around suffering. I didn't know I had a choice in releasing pain and suffering. I thought it was what I was supposed to do in order to be accountable to myself, my family, and God.

My mentor who died a few years ago told me once, *"Jennifer, the last thing I gave up is suffering."* That sounded like a foreign language. Those words made me think. They opened a window to freedom that I didn't even know it was possible to choose.

Let me ask you a few questions. Read the question, close your eyes, and reflect on the question for three to five minutes:

- Do you believe that you have to be perfect? Why? Why not?
- Do you believe that you should suffer? Why? Why not?
- Do you believe you deserve to suffer? Why? Why not?

You were created to let your unique light shine upon the world, to love and experience a full and rewarding life. Grief and loss slow everything down. When you make a decision to figure how to live again, to heal, to love yourself through the grief even if you don't know how, you can move forward, move beyond where you are, one small step at a time. Transformation begins when you give yourself permission to live again.

Transformation begins when you give yourself permission to live again.

- Would you be willing to let go of your pain? Why? Why not?
- What would happen if you let go of your guilt, shame, anger, and regret?
- What would your life look like if you let go of the belief that you have to suffer?

Your loved ones want you to be happy, be at peace, and to shine! They are loving and supporting you on your healing journey while you are in this world.

Fear comes up when you consider letting go of the pain. At least it did for me. I was worried what my loved ones and God might think about my choice. I believed at some level that if I held on to the pain, it was my way of showing my loved ones I loved them and that I would never let them go. Guilt protected me. I thought that if I remembered my guilt, it would never happen again. It was my way of letting my dad know I was sorry for letting him down. I held shame close for all my mistakes, thinking it was my atonement to God.

This was my mindset and my beliefs when I started my healing process. I've learned more and been able to let go a little bit at a time. It's been like peeling an onion. One layer at a time.

My healing process began with three simple decisions:

- I decided to learn how to live again.
- I made a commitment to be kinder to myself, to heal my heart and mind.
- I opted for the philosophy that small steps are enough. Less than perfect was okay.

You may be further along in your path of self-love and healing. Let me congratulate you for a job well done. Keep moving forward. There are better days ahead.

If you are feeling guilty for wanting to move on or are afraid of what your loved ones will think, it's okay. You won't forget them or disrespect them. In fact, they want to help us find peace and enjoy our lives while we are here. I'm not just saying this to make you feel better. I've heard loved ones share this in the readings I've done for clients and students. On a personal level, my dad went to great lengths to get my attention and let me know it was okay with him. Your loved ones want the same for you.

Consider this:
- What if it was you in the Spirit World?
- What would you want to give to your loved ones struggling with guilt, regret, sadness, depression, or anger?

When you let go of the pain and struggle a little bit at a time, your inner light, your inner Spirit shines. Your vibration is higher and you feel better. You're going to be better able to feel your loved ones when they stop by for a visit. When your vibration is high, you feel more at ease and are stronger. Your inner light starts shining, and hope arrives. That is good news for them and for you! You deserve it. You are enough and you are worth it.

If you are feeling guilty for wanting to move on or are afraid of what your loved ones will think, it's okay.

Strategy 1, *giving yourself permission*, is a powerful decision and action in your healing journey. I hope you incorporate it in your life. It is an act of self-love.

The exercise for this chapter is writing a note to yourself. You'll give yourself permission to take one step forward in your healing journey. I've included an example with suggestions and prompts to inspire you. Feel free to write your letter using the prompts provided in the example worksheet included or create your own letter.

It may be helpful for you to know what I wrote down for myself:

1) For things that I will give myself permission to do:
    - I wrote that I would give myself permission to take a singing class.
    - I'm also going to give myself permission to stop feeling afraid.
2) I'm willing to let go of fear of tomorrow and focus on staying present in today.
3) In pursuit of my healing, I am willing to:
    - Go back to church and do my meditations on a regular basis
    - Forgive
    - Take a dance class
    - Get out of my comfort zone
4) My phrase is *"What I don't know, I can learn."*
5) I'm going to look back at all I've done this month and celebrate my progress.
6) I'm going to ask the Spirit World to help me.

After my mom died, I gave myself permission to heal. I decided to be kind to myself. While moving through grief, I gave myself permission to change and let go of my long-standing beliefs that sabotaged my healing process. The biggest change for me was letting go of the need to be perfect in all things. It was one of my old beliefs. Perfectionism gave me a false sense of control and safety. If I could be perfect, I would be enough, lovable, safe and secure in this world. It has taken me a long time to let the need to be perfect go. Attempting to achieve perfection was self-defeating. I put myself through a lot of pain, stress and anxiety trying to achieve the idea of perfection. In deciding to heal and be kind to myself, loving and accepting myself has been and still is a top priority in my healing journey. I've made great progress in this area over time.

> *Other words could be terms like compassion, self-love, courage, peace, abundance, healing, forgiveness, and joy.*

Here are some of the new beliefs that I've been applying in my life:
- I am lovable.
- It is okay to ask for help.
- Less than perfect is okay.
- Taking days off is good for me.
- It is okay not have all the answers.
- Expressing my emotions is healthy.
- Gratitude relieves my pain and struggle.
- It is safe to let go of things that no longer serve me.
- Experimenting and learning new things helps me grow.
- When asked, *"Are you okay?"*, It is okay to say, *"No, but I'm learning how to deal with it."*

The exercise worksheet example includes setting intentions with a word or phase that empowers you. When I decide on a word or phrase to anchor my energy and focus, I ask Spirit to guide me and put words in my consciousness. I get quiet and calm for five to ten minutes. Then I make a list of words and phrases that come to mind.

Once I have a list of words and phrases, I ask my Higher Self to help me pick the best word or phrase that will help express my Higher Self. I select a word or phrase that resonates with me. I take time at the beginning of each year when setting goals and intentions for the upcoming year. Feel free to experiment with this process daily, weekly or monthly. As you

Love lives on and we can experience it more fully if we are open to receive it.

grow and heal, your needs and intentions will change. It's fun and gets easier with practice. This process will help you focus on your intentions and raise your energy higher with practice.

Words and phrases for me over the years:

- Grow with ease
- Achieve
- Love
- Service
- Accomplish
- Get comfortable in the uncomfortable
- Give with a happy heart
- It's safe to love

Other words could be terms like compassion, self-love, courage, peace, abundance, healing, forgiveness, and joy.

Begin the day by saying the word or phrase that resonates with you or the word Spirit has put in your consciousness. Saying this word will help you get through the day and make it easier to be your Higher Self. You can finish the sentence in a different way, with whatever issue is on your mind. Saying this word will make it easier…to pay my bills…to have confidence in myself…to let go of worry. Choose whatever feels right to you.

What do you want to look back and celebrate? This is an important step in healing. Honoring and celebrating wins no matter how big or small is very important. It helps improve self-esteem, confidence, and inner strength. It motivates and urges you to keep your progress moving forward. It also keeps you accountable no matter how long it takes. It will encourage you to follow through, to reach your dream and goals.

Think of the phrase *"Be true to you."*

At the start of 2017, I committed to learning how to create an online workshop to help people heal with the Spirit World. I was super excited to do it. I took a leap of faith and I signed up for a master program to help me professionally write and produce the online workshop. The master class was intense. It forced me to get out of my comfort zone. Right when I was making progress in the master program and putting the workshop together, my mom died.

A few weeks after her funeral, I made a decision to complete what I started. In fact, it gave me a reason to get out of bed in the morning. I had the presence of mind to think ahead. To decide how I wanted to grieve. The miracle in her death was that my mom helped me teach what was possible to others. She showed up many times in my dreams and in my daily life that year with message of encouragement and love. I was able to share her visits with my students. Some of my presentations were less than perfect, for sure. I held it together as best I could. While teaching several classes, I got emotional and cried when I least expected it. I know she loved being part of the process. We got to work on the project together. I can look back on that year and celebrate my progress and the love she shared with me. Love lives on, and we can experience it more fully if we are open to receive it.

Think about who you are going to reach out to, who you are going to tell about your commitment to yourself. Maybe that means committing to seeing a counselor, to writing in a journal, maybe to doing your spirit guide meditation more often, or reaching out to like-minded friends who will be supportive of you being your Higher Self.

Okay, now it's your turn.

Instructions:
1) Make sure you won't be disturbed for the next half hour.
2) Have a pen, paper or journal ready.
3) Read over the example letter and exercise.
4) Download and print the example letter and worksheet.
5) Reflect on each suggestion.
6) Create a list of things that could go in your letter.
7) When you're ready, write your letter.
8) Read it over and make any changes.
9) Now read the letter out loud to yourself, preferably in front of a mirror.
10) When reading your letter in front of the mirror, take a few seconds before and after to get centered and look upon your reflection in the mirror with kind and compassionate eyes.
11) If you opt to read it out loud without the mirror, put your hand over your heart. By using the mirror or holding your hand on your heart, reading it out loud, you are demonstrating your truth, showing respect to yourself and honoring your journey. It is a journey only you can take.
12) Read and review your letter once a day for the next two weeks. Once you complete the two weeks, review it often for the next three months. Update it at least once a year.

EXERCISE 3

GIVING YOURSELF PERMISSION

Love Letter to Me

Dear _____,

I give myself permission to…

Example: Smile, move forward, try new things, etc.

In pursuit of healing, I am willing to…

Example: To meditate, forgive, let go of regret, be less than perfect.

Each day I will begin the day with saying these words or phrases. By saying these words or phrases, it will help me get through the day and make it easier.

Examples: I can do it. It's safe to take one step forward. Yes, I'm getting through it, progress is good enough. I love myself enough to do this.

I will look back and celebrate my progress and wins no matter how small.

I am so committed to this personal journey that I am going to reach out to…

Examples: God, Loved Ones, Spirit Guides, Friends, Mentor, Counselor, Community, etc.

asking for their love, support and friendship to help me heal.

It's OK that I don't have it all figured out yet. I'm going to persevere.

Now is the time for me to put me first, to grow, heal and learn to live again.

I know God and my loved ones are with me.

I am not alone. I have support.

Love, _____

WORKSHEET 4

YOUR LOVE LETTER TO YOURSELF:

WORKSHEET 4

YOUR LOVE LETTER TO YOURSELF:

WORKSHEET 5

YOUR PERSONAL REFLECTIONS:

_____
_____
_____
_____
_____
_____
_____
_____
_____
_____
_____

QUESTIONS FOR JENNIFER:

_____
_____
_____
_____
_____
_____
_____
_____
_____

CHAPTER 3

Plan for stormy Weather

Bad weather happens. It's inevitable! And when it does, things turn out so much better when we plan for it ahead of time. I live in Florida. As hurricane season comes along, we know there may be storms ahead. We stock up on bottled water. We make sure to have plenty of batteries and flashlights on hand. When the storm comes, it can be scary, but we know we are ready. Grief, just like the weather, has seasons. There are dates and occasions on the calendar that trigger grief and can be more difficult. You can put a plan together ahead of time to handle the rough days that may lie ahead.

Maybe for you it's Thanksgiving, Christmas, or an anniversary, birthday, Mother's or Father's Day, the date of a divorce, the day your loved one died. As time passes, these dates and occasions can come and seem to stall or even reverse your healing progress. The good thing is, we know they're coming! We can prepare. We can plan ahead.

Grief just like the weather, has seasons too. There are dates and occasions on the calendar that we can predict ahead of time that things may get tough.

Thanksgiving and Christmas were a big deal for my family. After my mom died, instead of staying home, feeling sorry for myself, and allowing sadness and depression to take me down, I decided to plan ahead to get out and do things. I got a Disney pass. I'm not a regular Disney person. I was a little uncomfortable buying the pass because crowds overwhelm me. Planning to spend the day in a crowded park was 100 percent new for me. More importantly, I wanted to put myself in an uplifting environment. I wanted to be a good example for my son and daughter-in-law on how to handle grief in a positive way. I know someday my day will come to cross the rainbow bridge, and I want my son to take care of himself and have joy in his life. It felt good having a plan for the dates that I knew were going to be especially tough for me.

On one of my visits to Disney, I invited my mom to be there and enjoy it with me. I was overjoyed when I recognized a couple signs from her. I knew she was there! Two awesome things happened: 1) I felt comforted by her presence, and 2) she was able to enjoy things with me that she was not able to do on this side. She was disabled for much of her life, and for the first time, she got to go out and see the world with me.

Another date that weighed on my mind months before the actual day was my son's wedding day. My mom and son were very close. She was thrilled her only grandchild was getting married. She loved him and his wife-to-be so much. She could not travel, so we planned to have the wedding recorded and streamed live so she could watch and enjoy from her home in Texas. She died before the wedding day. Her presence would be greatly missed on their special day.

I was worried that I would have an uncontrollable crying episode in the middle of the wedding when reminded of her absence. My only plan was to invite her to join us for the wedding from Heaven. On the day of the wedding, I said a little prayer to my mom, asking her to be there and to give us a sign. I told my son and his wife-to-be that I knew she would be sending her love from Heaven. I was not sure what kind of

For all of us going through a loss, there is empty space left behind where a loved one once gave us energy and love. Now we need to fill those empty spaces their absence has left us with.

sign we would receive. I just trusted that she heard me.
After the wedding ceremony and reception, my son and his beautiful wife went out on the grounds to get pictures made. When he returned, he told me a lone butterfly had followed them around while the photographer was taking pictures. When he told me, I was comforted, overjoyed, and relieved all at the same time. We all knew the butterfly was the sign from my mom that she was with us on his special day.

Though I had been worried about crying at the wedding, I only cried for a few moments before, during, and after the wedding. The moments were shorter than expected, though. In spite of my own grief, I was present and available for my family on a very important date.

I have accepted grief will come and go in my life. It does not matter how long ago the passing happened. When I think about the important dates and events to come, remembering my loved ones who are not physically with me, I feel overwhelmed with grief. Fear comes over me. I start to worry about how hard grief might hit me and if I will be able to handle it. When I put a plan in place ahead of time, my feelings of overwhelm and grief lessen significantly. I feel stronger and confident that I can handle whatever comes on the day.

The truth is, these calendar days or special occasions will be different for you. Things have changed and will be new for you. If you take the time to plan ahead you will be helping your healing process in a big way. You will save yourself a lot of heartache and pain. The fear and anticipation of the coming day or occasion is often times worse than the actual day. Not having a plan in place could derail all the healing progress you have made. If you have a plan in place for that day, then you don't have to worry or get overwhelmed in thinking about how you are going to handle it. You have a plan ready and you know how you want to spend your day. You are ready!

For all of us going through a loss, there is an empty space left behind where a loved one once shared energy and love with us. Now we need to fill those empty spaces.

In the exercise below, you'll create a stormy weather plan. It does not have to be a definite plan, and you can change or update it at any time. The important part is to acknowledge the potential of rough days ahead. You will be able to handle it. You will be ready if they come.

Maybe you can plan to spend the day with a friend, go golfing, go to the beach, go out for dinner, or sign up to volunteer somewhere. Choose an activity that is fun for you and that makes you happy. Try something different, something new, more than sitting at home. You can invite your loved ones to join you. Think about the calendar days ahead, those trigger moments, that you know will bring up emotional bad weather. Work on your stormy weather plan.

The plan is not a cure-all. It doesn't make the hurricane of grief go away, but it makes getting through the hurricane or the smaller storms a little more bearable.

EXERCISE 4

PREPARING FOR THOSE DAYS

There are days in the calendar year that can be extra hard to get through because they are reminders of loss, no matter how long it's been since the loss happened. Just thinking about the marked dates and occasions can bring up painful feelings of grief.

For many people, these dates are the dreaded reminders of loss, regrets and loneliness. When the actual date arrives on the calendar, sadness and depression can take hold of the day and leave you reliving the pain again.

Part of starting the healing process is realizing and accepting that there will be difficult times, days and weeks ahead. You are in a

Storm of Change — you will get through it!

The fear of how you are going to handle tough times like birthdays, anniversaries, Father's Day, Mother's Day, the date of the death, and so many more is usually far worse than the actual day itself. By planning for the stormy weather days, you'll have a self-care plan in place when the day arrives.

WORKSHEET 6

STORMY
WEATHER PLAN

WHAT DATES AND EVENTS INTENSIFY FEELINGS OF GRIEF AND LOSS?

_____
_____
_____
_____
_____
_____

WHAT DATES OR DAY-TO-DAY THINGS TAKE PLACE DURING THE NEXT THREE TO SIX MONTHS THAT COULD TRIGGER GRIEF? LET'S MAKE A STORMY WEATHER PLAN TOGETHER!

EXAMPLE:

MONTH: *December*

TOUGH DATE: *Christmas Eve*

GAME PLAN: *Volunteer at a local animal shelter*

1.

MONTH: _____

TOUGH DATE: _____

GAME PLAN: _____

2.

MONTH: _____

TOUGH DATE: _____

GAME PLAN: _____

WORKSHEET 6

EXAMPLE:

MONTH: *July*

TOUGH DATE: *Spouse's Birthday*

GAME PLAN: *Make plans to have dinner with friends*

3.
MONTH: _____

TOUGH DATE: _____

GAME PLAN:

4.
MONTH: _____

TOUGH DATE: _____

GAME PLAN:

5.
MONTH: _____

TOUGH DATE: _____

GAME PLAN:

6.
MONTH: _____

TOUGH DATE: _____

GAME PLAN:

7.
MONTH: _____

TOUGH DATE: _____

GAME PLAN:

WORKSHEET 6

EXAMPLE:

MONTH: *July*

TOUGH DATE: *Spouse's Birthday*

GAME PLAN: *Make plans to have dinner with friends*

8.

MONTH: _____

TOUGH DATE: _____

GAME PLAN: _____

9.

MONTH: _____

TOUGH DATE: _____

GAME PLAN: _____

10.

MONTH: _____

TOUGH DATE: _____

GAME PLAN: _____

11.

MONTH: _____

TOUGH DATE: _____

GAME PLAN: _____

12.

MONTH: _____

TOUGH DATE: _____

GAME PLAN: _____

WORKSHEET 7

YOUR PERSONAL REFLECTIONS:

_____
_____
_____
_____
_____
_____
_____
_____
_____
_____
_____
_____
_____
_____

QUESTIONS FOR JENNIFER:

_____
_____
_____
_____
_____
_____
_____
_____
_____
_____
_____

CHAPTER 4

Rest, Repair and Rebuild

When we're struggling through fear, loss, and grief, *"pushing through"* is not necessarily the answer. During this struggle, we need extra amounts of self-care, not less. We need more permission to tend to our needs, not less. We need more self-love, not self-criticism.

When we've had the life force energy sucked out of us because of a big disappointment or loss, we need rest. We need to sleep longer. We need to go to bed earlier. We need to unplug from technology. Getting massages, playing with pets, spending time with children, friends, grandchildren, getting energy healings, listening to uplifting music, taking walks in nature, doing yoga, or writing in a journal are all actions you can take that help in the rebuilding process. After loss, everything changes. We need time to get our footing.

During this struggle, we need extra amounts of self-care, not less. We need more permission to tend to our needs, not less. We need more self-love, not self-criticism.

My mom died a few years ago. I flew back to Texas a couple of days after I got the call to take care of her final wishes. I handled her finances and planned the funeral. My family was there to support me, and God helped me. I was in shock and put a lot of pressure on myself to do everything perfectly. Once everything was taken care of, I flew back to Florida. I did not get off the couch for three straight days. I didn't talk to anyone and just binge-watched TV. Even now, I can't remember what I watched.

I made a decision while I was resting to love myself more, that I would give myself a break while grieving. I did not get through my dad's passing well and caused myself a lot of damage. This time, I wanted to handle grief differently. I committed to being kinder to myself. I was not going to pretend everything was fine. I surrounded myself with safe and supportive friends and family. When I needed rest, I rested. When I felt like crying, I cried. When I was angry, I expressed it. When I was sad, I didn't hold it in. When I missed her, I wasn't afraid to tell people. A lot of blessings came about after mom's death. I sense she is proud of me and how I have handled it this time around. I realized my feelings are just feelings. They will not kill me. If I honor my feelings and am willing to be present with them, they pass through me with more ease. I allow myself to grieve, regardless of the time or place. The good news is that I have kept my personal commitment to myself to walk through grief with courage, kindness and honesty. I know when I need rest or need to nurture myself with a day off, relaxing baths, naps, and massages. I'm not afraid to say I miss my mom or talk about her when I sense others think I should be over it by now.

After a loss, we need to repair. This is something more than just repairing our energy. For example, one thing I needed to repair was the overwhelming guilt and regret that I carried inside of me regarding my dad and his passing. You see, my dad and I were very close. He was my *"daddy"* and I was his angel baby. He was the one person I knew believed in me and loved me no matter what screw ups or mistakes I made. He would always be there for me.

He was also a chronic alcoholic and suffered from severe post-traumatic stress syndrome from his time in the Navy. He had been in and out of treatment centers too many times to count. He had no interest in or desire to get sober. One thing that comes from living with an alcoholic is a lot of unhealthy coping mechanisms. Growing up with an alcoholic is a roller coaster of unexpected twists, turns, high highs and lower lows. It's like walking on eggshells, being afraid to make a wrong move that will bring on another binge. In my home, we had house rules and expectations like don't rock the boat, keep the family secret, don't get your hopes up, don't talk about what's really going on, and pretend like everything is okay.

I loved my dad more than life itself, even when he was drunk. Watching him drink himself to death 24 hours a day became too difficult. I dreaded going to see him. One day, while I was at work, he called me out of the blue and asked me to come and see him. I found the courage to tell him that I could not see him while he was drinking, that it was too hard to see him like that. He died the next day. I was devastated. The earth fell from beneath my feet. My heart shattered into a million little pieces. I was almost twenty years old. I felt responsible for his death. If I had only gone to see him, he would have lived. I couldn't handle the reality of his death. I felt guilty that I was not there for him, that he had died alone, feeling rejected by his only daughter. What were his last thoughts? Did he know how much I loved him even with all his faults? For years, I felt like I had disappointed him by not going over and that broke his heart. I remember a secret promise I made at his funeral: I would never love or get close to anyone again.

After his death, I experienced intense anger, denial, and depression. It took me down a road of self-destructive living where I wished for the end. I made a plan to end my life one night. Thankfully, God sent an Angel to help me and my plan was put on pause.

Somewhere deep inside I found the will to live with the pain. I stayed in grief for a very long time because I did not know another way. I quietly repressed my anger at him for drinking, dying, and abandoning me. Guilt and regret became my inner voice repeating and reliving the circumstances around his passing. I expected perfection from myself in everything because I was angry at myself for not going to see him. Workaholism helped numb the pain of sadness and disappointment. I experienced all five stages of grief in my dad's passing – for many years.

Forgiveness is a powerful healer. Forgiving myself, God, and my dad did not happen overnight. It has come in stages. I've made huge progress, even when I have experienced grief again. Now I reach for self-love and compassion. I don't have to suffer and punish myself by staying in guilt and regret. My hope is that I get better and better over time when I think about the choices and decisions I've made in my life. I let the grief, regret, and guilt rise to the surface without trying to change, deny, or repress it. I give it space to breathe. It's the beauty of my humanness. I use positive phrases and remind myself, that I did the best I could with what I knew at the time.

My first step toward forgiveness was believing in myself. Little by little, I looked at myself in the mirror hoping to like and love the person looking back. I knew that I was smart and could solve life problems. I sought out personal growth and self-help books to guide me in solving my emotional problems. I also believed that the power of love could heal, that God would help me find peace within myself. One of the most profound gifts that helped me with forgiveness was an unexpected visit from my dad. It came more than ten years after his passing. During my repairing and rebuilding process, I found an internet radio station featuring a bunch of different authors and speakers. One day I felt the urge to call in and talk to a guy who could talk to loved ones on the other side. I was skeptical, but I felt pulled to call in anyway. I'd learned over the years to trust my intuition and follow my instincts. It was an important part of my healing process.

There were only a couple of minutes left in the show when I finally got the courage to call in. I was afraid to get my hopes up. In dealing with my dad, it brought up so much pain. I was not sure I could handle another disappointment. With all the healing work I'd done, grief could still bring me to my knees.

When I made the call, I thought about my dad. I said out loud, *"Daddy, if this is possible and you can really do this, now is the time. I may not have the courage to call in again."* I'd almost given up.

The host of the show was closing the show. At the very last minute, he said, *"I have time for one more."* He came on and said, *"I got your dad here with me. He says, 'It's okay, baby. It's okay.'"*

A river of tears rolled down my face. My dad shared a message for my brother, too: "Happy Birthday, DJ." My dad called my brother DJ. I knew it was my dad.

I didn't get to say goodbye. I was not there for him when he died. Somehow my dad found a way to talk through the host of the show. My dad's message, *"It's okay, baby,"* was exactly what I needed to hear. I knew it was my dad, I felt it in my heart.

In less than a minute, years of grief and regret melted upon hearing the messages from my dad. I'm convinced my dad's love for me came through at the exact time and in the exact way needed to heal my heart. My dad showed up and taught me that love never dies, that the Spirit World wants us to heal and be at peace.

Since that time, I've devoted my life to serving the Spirit World. Our loved ones, Spirit Guides, Angels, and God will go to great lengths to heal us if we allow ourselves to stay open to receive their love.

> *I had to repair my coping mechanisms. I had to take time to learn and build a new perspective, a new way and a new lens through which I looked at life.*

For me to be happy and experience joy again, I had to repair how I dealt with life. It has taken a lot of courage and work. I had to repair my coping mechanisms. I had to take time to learn and build a new perspective, a new way and a new lens through which I looked at life.

- I had to repair how I thought about myself and life.
- I had to rebuild my faith in God.
- I had to learn it was safe to love and get close to people. That was so hard for me – to let my guard down and get close to people again. I was afraid that if I got too close to people, that they would leave or die.

Learning how to live with loss includes reframing and rebuilding your life, while being open to learn and create a new perspective. It's okay to want to move forward and rebuild. You are not disrespecting or dishonoring your loved ones. Trust me, you won't forget them. Once you love someone, you always love them. Your loved ones will be with you as you reframe and rebuild your life if you are open to it.

One of my favorite quotes I read early on in my growth had a lasting positive effect on my life. Dr. Wayne Dyer said, *"When you change the way you look at things, the things you look at change."* His message gave me permission to let go of the pain. It gave me hope that I could be at peace. Feeling supported by others and being surrounded by like-minded friends is a huge part of this rebuilding of our new selves.

The Spirit within is always nudging you toward love and wholeness. It's always supporting you with unconditional love. It doesn't require perfection from you.

Finding a cause can be a very fulfilling way to rebuild your life. All you need is one purpose. It doesn't have to be huge. It doesn't have to be a whole-life change in every part of your life. You've already been through that change. Starting with small baby steps is the best way to begin. Setting up a daily or evening prayer or meditation ritual could be instrumental in healing. Hobbies like music, growing plants, caring for animals or grandkids on a weekly basis could be the start. Exercise is a great way to nurture yourself and rebuild your body and Spirit. I know a lot of people who have found a new purpose in their life after their loved one passed by volunteering and working with animals. The opportunities are endless. You are worthy of love and forgiveness. Healing yourself and rebuilding your life could be your first purpose. Make a decision to believe that peace and joy are possible.

What part of your life do you want to repair, rebuild, or make new again?

We can't force change. We grow into it. The will and strength to live comes from the Spirit within you. Within you is a force of love and strength. The Spirit within is always nudging you toward love and wholeness. It's always supporting you with unconditional love. It does not require perfection from you. You don't have to prove anything. All it asks of you is to make the time and space to get quiet and connect. The Spirit within you wants the best for you. It's important to honor its inner nudges to heal, move forward, and make slow, steady progress in rebuilding your life.

For the exercises that follow, allow yourself to think about what you can do, what actions you can take to nurture your mind, body, and emotions and start reframing and rebuilding your life. I've added a gratitude and forgiveness worksheet to help you get started. You don't have to do all the exercises at once. You can start with one that calls to you and do it for a week or a month. Review your progress once a month for the next three months. Celebrate your wins. There is no need to beat yourself up if you didn't meet your goal. Just start again, with one or two actions when you are ready.

Be compassionate to yourself, like you would treat a close friend.

Applying the strategies and working on the exercises in this book will help you get started. You don't have to rush through everything. Take it slow and steady, allowing time for rest and breaks. Go easy on yourself. Your healing is in your hands, and you can work at a pace that's right for you. Be compassionate to yourself, like you would treat a close friend.

EXERCISE 5

REST, REPAIR AND REBUILD

In dealing with grief, extra amounts of self-care and Spirit nurturing activities are essential in the healing process. There are many activities that you can do that will help recharge and replenish you.

Some examples include:
- Relaxing yoga practice, meditation, spending time in nature
- Hot baths, using essential oils, getting a massage
- Taking afternoon naps, unplugging from the Internet, turning off the TV
- Spending time with loving friends or pets, taking a weekend trip, reading a book
- Daily gratitude journal, self-forgiveness practice, counseling
- Writing or reciting prayers, creating and practicing affirmations, reading a book
- Research and get a new hobby, job, or project

Putting yourself first may be new for you. Your needs are important. *REPLENISHING YOUR MIND, BODY AND SPIRIT OFTEN BRINGS COMFORT AND FEEDS YOUR SOUL.*

For this exercise, please select two or three activities that sound or feel right and healing to you. The important thing is to get started. Experiment with new self-care activities. Select at least one daily, weekly and monthly activity for the next 30 days. Refer to the examples above for ideas and inspiration to create your own list.

WORKSHEET 8

REST: WHAT ACTIVITIES CAN I START THAT WILL HELP ME RELAX AND REST?

Consider your mental, emotional, spiritual and physical wellbeing. Examples include:

- I'm being so hard on myself. I'm giving that a rest. I put a lot of stress on making everything perfect. I'm going to learn how to love and accept myself more.
- I'm stressing myself out all the time thinking so much. I'm going to practice staying in the moment more.
- I'm tired all the time. I can't get to sleep or stay asleep. I'm going to get a meditation and look up essential oils that will help me sleep better.
- Look up best essential oils and remedies for relaxation this week. Go to the park three times a week to watch ducks and relax.

WRITE A LIST OF THINGS YOU WOULD LIKE TO EXPERIMENT WITH TO HELP YOU RELAX AND REST.

_____   _____
_____   _____
_____   _____
_____   _____
_____   _____

MY PLAN TO REST AND RELAX: _____

_____
_____
_____
_____
_____
_____

WORKSHEET 8

_____
_____
_____
_____
_____
_____
_____
_____
_____

I NEED TO DO THIS BECAUSE:

_____
_____
_____
_____
_____
_____
_____
_____
_____
_____
_____
_____

DATE I AM GOING TO START: _____

DATE TO CHECK MY PROGRESS: _____

WORKSHEET 8

RECORD YOUR PROGRESS AND FOLLOW UP NOTES HERE:

WORKSHEET 8

REPAIR: WHERE DO I NEED REPAIR?

Consider your mental, emotional, spiritual and physical wellbeing. Examples include:
- Writing in my journal five things I'm grateful for every day starting today.
- I'm anxious and worried about so many things, so I'm going to practice deep breathing to help me relax and stay in the moment.

WRITE A LIST OF THINGS YOU WOULD LIKE TO START REPAIRING IN YOUR LIFE.

There is no right or wrong. List as many as you like. You do not have to start them all at once.

_____   _____
_____   _____
_____   _____
_____   _____
_____   _____

WHAT WOULD YOU LIKE TO START REPAIRING FIRST?

_____
_____
_____
_____
_____
_____
_____
_____
_____

WORKSHEET 8

I NEED TO DO THIS BECAUSE:

_____
_____
_____
_____
_____
_____
_____
_____
_____
_____
_____
_____

DATE I AM GOING TO START: _____

DATE TO CHECK MY PROGRESS: _____

WORKSHEET 8

RECORD YOUR PROGRESS AND FOLLOW UP NOTES HERE:

_____
_____
_____
_____
_____
_____
_____
_____
_____
_____

IS THERE ANYTHING IN YOUR LIFE THAT IS IN NEED OF REPAIR THAT YOU ARE NOT READY TO REPAIR YET? *Write it down. Make a personal commitment to start repairing when you are stronger.*

_____
_____
_____
_____
_____
_____
_____
_____
_____

WORKSHEET 8

REBUILD: WHAT PART OF MY LIFE WOULD I LIKE TO REBUILD?

Rebuilding is a longer process This is a new chapter of living. Life asks you to live a new normal. Get comfortable with being uncomfortable. You will get through it. Take it one day at a time. Examples include:

- I don't like going out to eat alone. I'll find a place I really like and go next week.
- I feel lost on Saturdays. We use to talk on the phone after I got off work. I am going to treat myself to a nice meal at the natural grocery store for a while.
- Learn how to let go of anger and practice forgiveness. Write God a letter about my anger for taking my dad away from me. Research and order a book about forgiveness next week.

WRITE DOWN A FEW THINGS THAT YOU ARE READY TO START REBUILDING:

There is no right or wrong. List as many as you like. You do not have to start them all at once.

_____   _____
_____   _____
_____   _____
_____   _____

WHAT WOULD YOU LIKE TO START REBUILDING FIRST?

_____
_____
_____
_____
_____

WORKSHEET 8

MY PLAN TO REBUILD:

_____
_____
_____
_____
_____
_____
_____
_____
_____
_____
_____

I NEED TO DO THIS BECAUSE:

_____
_____
_____
_____
_____

DATE I AM GOING TO START: _____

DATE TO CHECK MY PROGRESS: _____

WORKSHEET 8

RECORD YOUR PROGRESS AND FOLLOW UP NOTES HERE:

_____
_____
_____
_____
_____
_____
_____
_____
_____
_____

IS THERE ANYTHING IN YOUR LIFE THAT IS IN NEED OF REBUILDING THAT YOU ARE NOT READY TO REBUILD YET? *Write it down. Make a personal commitment to start rebuilding when you are stronger.*

_____
_____
_____
_____
_____
_____
_____
_____
_____

EXERCISE 6

FORGIVENESS OF SELF

Forgiveness is an essential action of the repair and rebuild healing phase. The blessing in forgiveness is freedom from the pain and hurt. It opens up a closed or injured part of the heart to experience love fully.

Our main purpose in life is to fearlessly give and receive love in healthy ways.

I know how to forgive others and for the most part, I forgive easily. My friend Mary Lou used to tell me, *"Jennifer, It is easy to love the lovable. It's harder to love the unlovable."* I could say that is also true for forgiveness.

Forgiving myself for things I felt I've done wrong has not been easy for me. Growing up, I thought if I could be perfect, I would be loved and accepted by God and the people in my life. I've had to learn how to forgive myself and people who have hurt or abandoned me in some way. It has gotten easier with practice. I learned very early on in life how to repress my feelings. Sometimes, I've been the last one to know I felt hurt or angry. I feel holding the hurt or judgment in my heart gives me a false sense of control over the situation.

I personally think everyone could benefit from the act of forgiveness because it allows more love on this earth.

For this exercise, write a forgiveness letter to yourself. Consider all the times you have expected perfection from yourself.

WORKSHEET 9

YOUR FORGIVENESS LETTER:

WORKSHEET 9

YOUR FORGIVENESS LETTER:

EXERCISE 7

GRATITUDE EXERCISE

Going through grief is not easy or fun. Practicing gratitude is a powerful tool when grieving. Sometimes we need help shifting our mind's focus off of what we have lost. Gratitude is the same as *"being thankful"* or *"having an appreciation for."* It is the expression of appreciation for what one has or had. It can bolster happiness and can play a major role in physical and psychological health. Practicing gratitude is a wonderful way to ease feelings of grief.

Gratitude can bring needed relief to painful thoughts and emotions. It can heal relationships with your loved ones in the Spirit World. I loved my mom and dad. Our family was dysfunctional. Alcoholism and addiction left a lot of wreckage in its path. When my mom and dad died, I had a lot of unresolved pain and hurt in my heart. Being grateful opened the door to forgiveness. Practicing gratitude and communicating with them in the Spirit World has helped me heal past hurts, resentments and regrets. Together, we have been able to heal a lot of the pain that we could not resolve here.

When you choose to be grateful, you are choosing love over pain.

Here are some examples of how you can express your gratitude:
- I am grateful for my past because it has made me strong and more caring about others.

- I am grateful that my dad has been freed from his alcoholism because he suffered with so much guilt from the war.

- I am grateful I had the strength to let go of the relationship that was not serving me.

WORKSHEET 10

DATE: _____

I am grateful for _____

because _____

_____

_____

DATE: _____

I am grateful for _____

because _____

_____

_____

DATE: _____

I am grateful for _____

because _____

_____

_____

DATE: _____

I am grateful for _____

because _____

_____

_____

DATE: _____

I am grateful for _____

because _____

_____

_____

WORKSHEET 10

DATE: _____

I am grateful for _____

because _____

_____

_____

DATE: _____

I am grateful for _____

because _____

_____

_____

DATE: _____

I am grateful for _____

because _____

_____

_____

DATE: _____

I am grateful for _____

because _____

_____

_____

DATE: _____

I am grateful for _____

because _____

_____

_____

WORKSHEET 11

YOUR PERSONAL REFLECTIONS:

_____
_____
_____
_____
_____
_____
_____
_____
_____
_____
_____
_____

QUESTIONS FOR JENNIFER:

_____
_____
_____
_____
_____
_____
_____
_____
_____
_____
_____

CHAPTER 5

Get a New Purpose

Our highest calling or purpose in life is to love and be loved in healthy ways. If grief goes unchecked it can keep you from fulfilling your highest calling and purpose. We are created with all we need to experience and live a full life. Human beings are perfectly equipped to handle all seasons of life. Just like the weather has four seasons, so do we. Instilled within each of us is an inner power, a life force energy. It is our survival instinct. It never gives up on us. It calls us to rise up and start again. It is a priceless gift. We have it so we can weather the storms and seasons of life.

You are meant to fearlessly live and love in all seasons. In grieving, loving yourself through the pain is the highest goal you can achieve. The life force energy within you will call you back to life after loss. The timing of this call is different for everyone. When you answer the call, you will be given the strength, will, and determination to go further than you think you can go. You were designed to express, create, produce and reproduce. It is part of who you are and what

When you connect with a new positive life-affirming activity, you reconnect with your ultimate purpose to love and be loved.

you came here to accomplish. When you get a new purpose, you create a season and are filled with renewed energy and focus.

Getting a new purpose and sticking with it for several months can get you out of the bed in the morning. It creates opportunity. It gives you a chance to experience life, love, and joy again. It creates new ideas and personal growth. It opens a window in a dark room. When you connect with a new, positive, life-affirming activity, you reconnect with your ultimate purpose to love and be loved.

- What new purpose is waiting for you?
- What have you been thinking about in the quiet moments of your day?
- What idea keeps coming to you?
- Is there something you want to learn, explore, or heal?
- Would you like to help others or volunteer?

Your soul is the quiet voice within you. It's been nudging you, trying to get your attention. It's been whispering to you, calling you to heal and connect to life again.

Finding a new purpose has a positively profound effect on grief. It does not remove the grief. Once you love someone, you'll always love the person. Finding a new purpose will strengthen you. It will increase your ability to adapt and accept life on life's terms. It helps manage depression. It restores hope, faith, and love.

Your soul is the quiet voice within you. It's been nudging you, trying to get your attention. It's been whispering to you, calling you to heal and connect to life again.

Learning something new, working through the first three strategies in this book, can be your purpose. Working through the heavy emotions of fear, loss, and grief is possible and is a big deal. It can sound intimidating. You may feel overwhelmed with the idea at first, worried that it's impossible to achieve. If you break the process into smaller chunks, you can do it! The hardest part is making a decision. It may feel scariest at the starting point, but the pay-off will be worth it if you follow through one small step at a time.

Just take that first baby step. **You don't have to wait to feel better.** Even that one first step can give you new energy. It can be as easy as writing a list of things that sound interesting. Then take one more step like researching, ordering a book, signing up for a class, picking up the phone and scheduling an appointment, or calling a friend.

Be kind and easy when you begin. Avoid putting pressure on yourself to complete your goal perfectly. Less than perfect is okay. If your purpose is a large project like starting a nonprofit organization, starting a support group, or writing a book, don't delay your reward until it is 100 percent completed. Celebrate each little baby step and action. You could end the day or week with a list of small accomplishments you completed like meditating, learning a new recipe, getting out of the house, or taking the dog for a walk. Grief can be debilitating at times, so just getting out of bed and eating a healthy meal every day is an accomplishment.

Don't wait to act out of fear that you won't finish. Even the action of research is a baby step – researching hobbies or groups or a new career. If it's a book you want to read or there is a book out there about something you're interested in, buying the book is a great first step. You don't have to read it right away to feel good about taking action, any action.

Part of your higher purpose is making your life work. Getting a new purpose opens the door to life again. It feels good to be productive and healthy.

After my mom died, my new purpose was to teach more. I knew that in order to be able to do that, I would need to learn how to better use the computer and how to build presentations. Knowing myself, I knew that learning process was not going to be easy for me. I was easily distracted, and I was still in shock about my mom's passing. I also suffered almost daily with migraine headaches. But I also trusted the little voice inside me that was telling me this was something I needed and wanted to do. To keep myself inspired, I picked a favorite song – *"Unstoppable"* by Sia. Every morning I would play that song and it would get me going on my learning process. Listening to it raised my energy and set the tone for the day. The lyrics and music were comforting and inspiring.

The other thing I did to keep me going on my new purpose was to plan a reward for myself. If you only make a list of your goals, it's sometimes hard to motivate yourself to take action. A list can be helpful as a reminder of the commitment you've made to yourself, but it can also be intimidating to look at. **Adding a reward makes taking that first step a little more enticing.**

For example, I told myself that if I could create a class and deliver a good product that would help my students, then I would give myself the gift of a weekend in the mountains. When I finished giving my first class, which I had worked extremely hard to create and prepare for, I did go to the mountains. I enjoyed that time to unplug and relax after all my hard work. My reward for writing this book is giving myself spa treatments at home.

Celebrate each baby step and then give yourself a reward for your accomplishment. It doesn't have to be as big as a trip to the mountains. If your new purpose is getting healthier by working out, your first baby step to celebrate can be deciding what you want to do or joining a gym. Set a goal of doing that activity or going three times a week and put it on your calendar. After you accomplish your first week, reward yourself with a new pair of workout socks or a fun water bottle. It doesn't have to be expensive. Part of your higher purpose is making your life work. Getting a new purpose opens the door to life again. It feels good to be productive and healthy.

Be a loving parent to yourself – don't just push, push, push. That doesn't usually work. Rewarding yourself for the effort every now and then feels good and keeps you motivated. There's an acknowledgment of celebration. Maybe you order something wonderful to eat or purchase a movie or buy a new CD. Maybe you go for a walk or take a drive and see a place you've always wanted to see. Create a reward to go with the building of your accomplishments. Consider a weekly or monthly goal to start.

It's okay to want to be happy and be at peace. Getting a new purpose can help you get there. God, your Spirit Guides, Angels, and your loved ones want to see you happy. They're happy for you. They are thinking, *"They finally did it!"* There is no need to feel guilty or worried. It's okay to move forward. They will be with you in their own unique way. Your loved ones are going to continue to support you and move forward with you.

God, your Spirit Guides, Angels, and your loved ones want to see you happy. They're happy for you. They are thinking, "They finally did it!"

You are important. Your life is important. You have something to offer this life. There is no right or wrong way to get a new purpose. The point is to find a purpose and follow through one day, one week, and one month at time. It can be simple. Self-love can be your purpose. Because, bottom line, we were created to love and be loved. That is the basic purpose of our physical life. When you begin to honor and recognize that, you are already making progress.

Your new purpose can be really simple—something that makes you feel love and joy and gives you positive energy. It doesn't have to be something as tangible as writing a book, starting a new business, or getting a new job or a hobby (but it can be!). It can be more personal, intangible, like self-care, healing, letting go of regrets, and working on the strategies in this workbook. Where in your life or within yourself can you add more love and give more love? Take a look at that. Let that be your purpose.

Get closer to your new purpose by working on the next exercise.

Where in your life or within yourself can you add more love and give more love?

EXERCISE 8

A NEW PURPOSE IN LIFE

It's okay to want to be happy and at peace.

Your loved ones WANT you to live and enjoy life on this side.

No need to feel guilty or worried that you might forget them if you move forward. They will be with you in their own unique way. You've already made a great start in your healing journey.

There is no right or wrong path in grief. Sometimes we get off track in our lives by events, loss and tragic circumstances, but your job is to know there are...

No Mistakes!

Little by little is the name of the game... Let's take baby steps together! Less than perfect is OK. We all have to start somewhere. Getting started is the hardest part.

IDENTIFY YOUR NEW PURPOSE!
Examples: Adopt an animal, start an exercise program, heal your body, connect more with Spirit, start a daily journal, write a book, go after that dream job, plan that missed vacation, or learn something new.

_____
_____
_____
_____
_____

WORKSHEET 12

YOUR NEW LIFE PURPOSE

SUMMARIZE: YOUR NEW PURPOSE HERE!

_____
_____
_____
_____
_____

MY KEY AREAS TO FOCUS ON INCLUDE:
Examples: Spiritual growth, mental and emotional well-being, physical health, nutrition, loneliness

1. _____

2. _____

3. _____

MY MONTH-AHEAD TO-DO LIST:
Examples: Get a new hobby, join a gym, research a mentor, decide on a counselor, sign up for a class, volunteer at the animal shelter

1. _____

2. _____

3. _____

WORKSHEET 12

PEOPLE YOU NEED TO REACH OUT TO INCLUDE:
Hint: Family, friends, trainer, counselor, mentor, email Jennifer

1.
2.
3.

THE SUPPORT AND LEARNING I WILL NEED INCLUDES:
Hint: Join Jennifer's Live sessions or watch replays/get a book/do exercises in this book

1.
2.

WHAT IS YOUR TIME FRAME AND REWARD:
Examples: Walk 30 minutes, 3x weekly – buy new colorful socks! Weekly meditation challenge – buy new meditation cushion or chair. Take a day off and spend at the park. Journal five minutes a day for 21 days – buy new colored pen and journal.

WORKSHEET 12

LET'S PLAN AHEAD.

Close your eyes and think about each one of your goals. Write one or two sentences that describe how your life will look or how you will feel when you achieve your goal.

_____
_____
_____
_____
_____
_____
_____
_____

HOW DOES IT FEEL NOW THAT YOU'VE MET YOUR GOAL?

_____
_____
_____
_____
_____
_____
_____
_____
_____
_____
_____
_____

WORKSHEET 13

YOUR PERSONAL REFLECTIONS:

_____
_____
_____
_____
_____
_____
_____
_____
_____
_____
_____
_____
_____
_____
_____

QUESTIONS FOR JENNIFER:

_____
_____
_____
_____
_____
_____
_____
_____
_____
_____
_____

CHAPTER 6

Connect to the Spirit World

When I learned to connect to the Spirit World, my life changed for the better in ways I could not have dreamed of. The Spirit World is the dimension we go to after we die. Some people refer to it as heaven, the other side or the afterlife. I believe it is the place we came from and the place where we will return when we die. It is our true home.

In my healing journey, I wanted to feel more connected to God, calm my racing mind and have some peace. A friend of mine suggested that I learn to meditate. When I started meditating, things began happening to me that I could not explain nor understand. When I would go for a walk or write in my journal, I felt an undeniable presence with me. It was comforting but unfamiliar. I did not know who or what

> *Doubt is a healthy response to an unknown that forces us to question our beliefs and the authenticity of our experiences.*

was with me. I felt like someone plugged me into a different channel that allowed me to see and feel an invisible world. Although I was not afraid, it was a little unsettling. I began having experiences with other people as well. One time while having a conversation with a co-worker, I could sense her mom who had recently died standing with us while we were talking.

A close friend from work suggested that I might have psychic abilities and that I consider exploring them more. She took the initiative to research schools that could help me. She found a highly regarded spiritualist school in England and recommended that I attend. I took a leap of faith. I requested a leave of absence from work, registered with the school and booked my airline ticket. The leave from work was approved and the school approved my registration. Flying to England was a new and exciting adventure. It was there that I was introduced to the Spirit World.

Attending the school was life changing for me. The tutors helped me understand what was happening to me. This was good news because it helped me adjust to my new level of understanding without feeling crazy. I learned so many things while I was at the school, far beyond what I was taught in church growing up. I learned we are pre-wired with the ability to connect and communicate with the Spirit World. We connect to the Spirit World through our Higher Self or Spirit Self. Some people refer to the Higher Self as their Spirit or soul.

Each of us has our own personal team of Spirit Guides, Angels, loved ones, and Ascended Masters who have always been there for us. They never leave us and they use every opportunity to support and protect us.

I wanted to learn everything I could, and I devoured the books in the school's library. I learned all I could about the Spirit World. I discovered our Spirit Team consists of our departed loved ones, Spirit Guides, Angels and Ascended Masters. This was very new to me. In my courses at the spiritualist school, we focused mainly on connecting with our Spirit Guides and developing our abilities. It was a big comfort and relief to learn that we all have this innate ability to communicate, that it is a God-given gift.

I found new hope in knowing that I was not alone. I was excited to think I could *"phone home"* to my Spirit Team whenever I needed help. They taught us that we all have a Spirit Team that loves, supports and guides us. It took some time for me to reconcile my belief and understanding of God and the Spirit World. For me, God is love and presides over everything including the Spirit World. Below are some key insights I learned and experienced when connecting to the Spirit World:

- It is open to all who seek.
- We all have Spirit Guides or helpers.
- Departed loved ones are on our Spirit Team.
- Our Spirit Team's mission is love, healing and evidence of the afterlife.
- There is nothing to fear when connecting to the Spirit World.
- We don't have to believe 100% to connect and communicate.

Connecting to the Spirit World and choosing to live a life that includes the Spirit World is not for everyone. We have all come across people who are skeptics or naysayers. I've seen the eye-rolling, read ugly posts, and been laughed at for my beliefs. That has not stopped me from pursuing my inspiration. Everyone is entitled to their own beliefs.

Some people have a belief system that will not allow them to consider or perceive any hint that they have access to the support of the Spirit World. They may cite a lack of scientific proof or specific religious teachings in an effort to discount that which they do not understand. It is okay to doubt. Doubt is a healthy response to an unknown that forces us to question our beliefs and the authenticity of our experiences. As such, this attitude of uncertainty and fear directly influences us in all matters. There is a wonderful saying that *"Doubt is fine for doubt's sake, but when it becomes a hindrance and blocks you in your personal and spiritual goals, it becomes a problem."*

Still, it is understandable that there may be some fears associated with the Spirit World. Commonly we grow up with scary stories of ghosts and demons. We experience, feel, and hear things that we do not fully understand. We scare ourselves with the unknown.

Know this: your connection with the Spirit World should not be frightening. The Spirits we are talking about are born of light and love and resonate in the higher frequencies. It is by the natural law of love that they can do no harm as they are born of love. Each of us has our own personal team of Spirit Guides, Angels, loved ones, and Ascended Masters who have always been there for us. They never leave us and they use every opportunity to support and protect us.

There is work and practice you will need to do to open yourself to the Spirit World connection so that you can utilize this most extraordinary resource. Throughout our cultures there is a stigma associated with those who work with the Spirit World. You may find yourself feeling secretive at first about your interest in the spiritual for fear of scorn from family and friends. The fear of how we are perceived forces many to go underground with new discoveries. This trend is changing as there is a global recognition of a spiritual connection. I created a private Facebook group, Solutions of Spirit, to help people connect and be supported by like-minded people.

I didn't always know that I had a Spirit Team or that I could get help from them. I didn't even know I had a Higher Self that could connect to Spirit. That knowledge was not something that was always there. I knew there was a God, but I was not sure he had been there for me. Gratefully now, I know I was being carried during my toughest moments.

It wasn't until I made my purpose spiritual growth and started meditating that I began to feel and sense other things with the Spirit World. That's actually how it happened for me. I didn't start off knowing that I could connect to my dad, Angels, and Spirit Guides. I was struggling from unresolved grief and fear and did not feel connected to this physical world. I wanted to calm my mind and feel closer to God, and the Spirit World opened up for me.

I started to meditate in the morning with five minutes on a kitchen timer. I made it a priority. It took me a lot of practice to be able to meditate. My mind was and still is at times like an air traffic control center, always sorting out my thoughts looking for a safe place to land. A friend gave me a book about energy, and I loved it. Then, I studied how to connect to my Spirit Guides. My inner senses heightened as I learned, and I began to feel people's energy and see their loved ones with them. One of the most noticeable things I felt over time was my vibration. As I connected with my higher self in my daily life, I felt charged up with new energy. It was as if I went from a 110-volt electric plug on a toaster to a 220-volt electric plug like a clothes dryer. That's actually how it started for me – at least that's the short version.

For over 25 years, I've been committed and devoted to healing with spirituality and deepening my relationship with God. Meeting a team of Angels, Spirit Guides, and loved ones was the bonus.

The Spirit World, our Angels, Spirit Guides, and loved ones are intelligent and understand the right timing for our healing. We simply have to be open to learn and grow. If you did not grow up knowing you could connect and communicate to the Spirit within, your Angels, Spirit Guides, and your loved ones, it's not too late. As I mentioned above, I didn't know about this other spiritual dimension either! I grew up in a fundamentalist Christian church. No one talked about the Spirit World on Sundays in church. It was something I had to discover and explore new on my own.

I believe connecting to the Spirit World is a gift from God, our birthright. It doesn't matter how old you are or what experiences you've had. You can at this very moment, at this very time, using what I'm sharing with you today in this guide, start to build your awareness and connection to the Spiritual World. It's best to begin by taking small steps. I started with a five-minute meditation before I began my day. You can start your own journey with the Spirit World a little at a time.

There is a pathway to the Spirit World. Start with being aware that you are more than a physical being, and that you have a Higher Self. It is the part of you connected to the Spirit World. Some people refer to this as your Spirit Self, the Higher Self, or your soul.

Do you believe or are you willing to believe that you are more than a physical being? Have you felt or sensed your loved ones or Angels with you? It's not just in your head or wishful thinking…they are letting you know that you are not alone. You don't have to believe 100 percent to make progress on your path. The Spirit World will meet you halfway.

Helping people learn how to connect and communicate with the Spirit World has been one of the best experiences of my life. I am able to see the Spirit World come alive in their lives, sharing in their pain and healing. I feel super excited when they have heard from a loved one or made a big breakthrough in their healing process.

To begin with Strategy 5, I suggest you make learning more about the Spirit World a goal for the next three months. Make it part of your purpose that we discussed in Strategy 4.
The first step in connecting to the Spirit World is opening your mind to the possibility.

You are already ahead of the game because you are here. The second step is to raise your energy and start to recognize your Higher Self. The fastest and easiest way to get started is with a guided meditation.

Meditation is such an important core basic skill if you want to overcome fear and anxiety and heal your heart and mind.

Meditation is something that has to be made a priority and it's a skill that you can develop. The cool thing is, there's no meditation police! You can really grow with your own style. I prefer to do my meditations in the morning. I sometimes use guided meditations and sometimes I use writing, but the goal is to re-center into that quiet place inside. Our interior world empowers us so that we can connect better in the outer world.

At the end of this chapter, you'll find the Strategy 5 Exercises and Meditations. I've included three meditations that you can use to start making your connection with the Spirit World. In that section, you'll find the printable meditation script and the link to the downloads:

- **Clear Your Mind Meditation** (11-minute mp3 download and written practice)
- **Mindful Meditation** (practice on your own)
- **Healing Grief Meditation** (15:48 minutes mp3 download and written practice)

Meditation is so essential and can be such a powerful and positive part of your healing that I want to discuss it in more depth and explain how it can benefit your life.

GUIDANCE FOR GETTING STARTED CONNECTING WITH THE SPIRIT WORLD

Meditation
Made Easy

Everyone can meditate. Explore what works best for you. For me, I can do about twelve minutes on my own. If I want more than that, I like guided meditations. They are great to start with because they take the guesswork out of the experience.

The main goal is to relax your body, gently focus on the words in the meditation, and let go of the outside world. Meditation raises your vibration and frequency. Raising your energy and vibration makes it so much easier to connect with the Spirit World. It also improves your overall well-being.

Meditation is a skill. Consistent practice accelerates your growth and you get better at turning down the mental noise. Release any expectations or needing to make something happen.

Let your goal be to show up, relax your body, gently focus your mind, and let go of

> *The main goal is to relax your body, gently focus on the words in the meditation, and let go of the outside world.*

BINGO

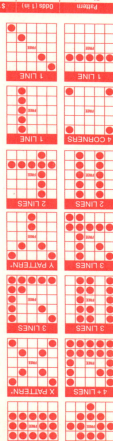

HOW TO PLAY
- Select the amount you would like to play per Bingo board.
- Select how many boards you would like to play per game.
- Select the number of consecutive games you would like to play.
  – A separate ticket will be randomly printed by the lottery terminal for each consecutive game.
- Multiply the number of games by dollars played per game by number of boards per game for your total wager amount.

HOW TO WIN
- Your Bingo board(s) will be randomly generated by the lottery terminal.
- Watch the monitor as 30 balls are drawn and land on the appropriate call numbers.
- Use these call numbers to create one of eight traditional Bingo patterns and win cash prizes.
- A winning line pattern can be located anywhere on the Bingo board (horizontal, vertical, or diagonal) but must include 5 matching call numbers or 4 call numbers and the FREE space.
- If more than one pattern is created on a Bingo board, the highest prize shall prevail.
* A winning Y or X Pattern must appear exactly as shown in the illustrations. No prize will be awarded for a Y or X Pattern in any other direction.

IMPORTANT
The ticket, not this slip, shall be the only valid proof of the selections made and the only valid proof for claiming a prize. Tickets may not be sold to persons under 18 years of age. Upon purchase of a ticket, players agree to abide by all the rules and regulations of the Rhode Island Lottery. Only patterns recognized as the official Rhode Island Lottery Bingo patterns shall be entitled to a prize.

PRIZE COLLECTION
Winners may claim prizes of $599 or less by presenting their winning tickets to any Rhode Island Lottery Retailer. Winners of more than $599 must claim their prizes at Rhode Island Lottery Headquarters, 1425 Pontiac Ave., Cranston, RI 02920. Telephone 401-463-6500.

BINGO PRIZES

Pattern	Odds (1 in)	$1 Prize	$2 Prize	$5 Prize	$10 Prize
Diamond	302,034	$10,000	$20,000	$50,000	$100,000
4 + Lines	12,903	$500	$1,000	$2,500	$5,500
X	2,990	$120	$240	$600	$1,200
3 Lines	1,524	$80	$160	$400*	$800
Y	347	$42	$84	$210	$420
2 Lines	94	$15	$30	$75	$150
4 Corners	49	$6	$12	$30	$60
1 Line	8	$1	$2	$5	$10
Overall	6.31				

Help is available for you or someone you know who has a gambling problem.
1-877-9-GAMBLE
Sponsored by the Rhode Island Lottery

RHODE ISLAND LOTTERY
www.RILOT.com
Tel. 401-463-6500
1425 PONTIAC AVE.
CRANSTON, RI 02920

RI-9011 RMF 09/12   E3   169431 RECYCLABLE

RHODE ISLAND LOTTERY

HOW TO PLAY AND WIN

Select the wager amount, the number of boards, and the number of consecutive games you want to play. Your Bingo board(s) will be randomly generated by the lottery terminal. You will receive a separate ticket for each consecutive game played. On the monitor, watch as 30 balls are drawn. Use these numbers to create the Bingo patterns listed to the right.

Prizes based on $1 wager

Pattern	Prize
Diamond	$10,000
4 + Lines	$500
X	$120
3 Lines	$80
Y	$42
2 Lines	$15
4 Corners	$6
1 Line	$1

- - - - - -
. . . .

1 How much do you want to play per board?
MARK ONE: ▭

$1 $2 $5 $10

2 How many boards do you want to play per game?
MARK ONE: ▭

1 2 3

3 How many consecutive games do you want to play?
MARK ONE: ▭

Multiply number of games by dollars played per game by number of boards per game for total wager.

1 2 3 4 5

the outside world. You can do this! A great meditation to start with is my Clear Your Mind meditation at the end of the chapter.

Every meditation practice is different. Some days you'll be able to relax, focus, and let go. Others...not so much. You get a gold star for showing up. Do your best to show up for your practice at the same time every day for seven days in a row and do the same practice. You can meditate in the morning or night – whatever works best for you. Try one of the three meditations at the end of the chapter for seven days and then try a different one for another seven. You'll know what is best.

There are three elements that you can assess as you grow in your meditation practice:

1) How good am I at relaxing my body? It took me a long time to learn to still my body.

2) Can I gently focus on following the guided practice or following the flow of my breath? Just because you can't shut your mind off doesn't mean you're not meditating well. The goal of meditation is not to turn off your mind. The mind is active. You are just changing the channel. Gently focusing improves concentration and new awareness.

3) How good am I at letting go of the outside world? Removing all distractions is important. When my son was a teenager, I meditated in my closet because there was so much going on in the house. Going in the closet and shutting the door helped me tell my mind, *"We are letting go of the outside world for ten minutes."*

Tuning into my Higher Self makes my head and heart happy. It's the one thing that has made my life whole and complete. I always say that, in my opinion, trying to live life without Spirit is like driving a car with four flat tires. You'll eventually get where you are going, but it's going to be a rough ride. With Spirit as your source and power, the tires are filled with energy and air so you can move easier, make turns, choose directions, and go places with more ease and flow.

When we only live in our left brain, which is where we think things out, we believe we can think our way through pain. I have had no luck trying to think my way through pain! But I have found that activating the right brain helps with all the over thinking that causes fear and self-doubt. Practicing right-brain activities like meditation, art, and free journaling helps awaken and rouse the Spirit within.

What has transformed and healed all areas of my life is connecting with the power of my own Spirit, with God, and with my spiritual energy and thoughts and feelings. The Spirit within you is like a seed waiting to be watered so it can grow and evolve within you and you can bloom in your life where you were dead before. Grief and loss and despair can make you dead. Connecting with your Higher Self and your Spirit Team can and will help bring you back to life.

Anyone can connect to the Spirit World. Give yourself permission to experience it without having to figure it all out in one day. Understand that it doesn't have to be perfect. You have permission to be healthy and find peace, to finally let go of guilt, to know that you are lovable enough as you are, that you have been a good parent, a good friend. There is nothing that you can do or say that would make you unworthy of having happiness and peace. You are the one who has to give yourself permission.

The truth is, the number one way to overcome fear, loss, grief, and struggle is to really decide that you want to handle things differently. You have made a big step in your healing process by putting some or all the five strategies to work for you.

A lot of people are afraid to let go of fear, loss, and grief. Living with grief can become our normal. Grief is the way that we go through our struggles. Sometimes it's all we've known. It is the way we connect to Spirit. Living with fear, loss, and painful feelings of grief is HOW we connect to life. It can help us feel connected to our loved ones. I stayed in the bargaining stage and anger for more than twelve years after my dad passed. At some level, I know it's how I felt close to him. But now, working through the ups and downs of grief and learning to connect with him in new ways, has been profoundly healing.

Let me assure you: **there is another way!**

It is okay to let go of the struggle. It is safe to move forward. Remember, the only thing that is changing is the way you are coping with life.

Once you start the process of letting go of the guilt (or even give yourself permission to let go of it for just 24 hours), there's a whole new space that you're giving God and Spirit to work within you. You're releasing some of the lower energy, the lower vibrations of guilt. You are clearing your psychic windshield so you can better see your new purpose. If you can be willing to forgive yourself, be willing to explore and experiment with new ideas and techniques, you can open up new space for new energy and love. No one is perfect. No one.

Hint: Go back to Strategy 3: Rest, Repair and Rebuild. Add an action or activity on your daily, weekly, or monthly plan.

These are just a few positive steps forward that you can take to start letting go of guilt:

- Take better care of yourself.
- Stop being so hard on yourself.
- Write a list of things you feel guilty about and write yourself a letter of forgiveness.
- Write a letter to your loved one in Spirit or God and ask for forgiveness. Keep in mind, you are already forgiven; the letter helps you acknowledge it and release it.
- Tell your inner bully or inner critic to be quiet.
- Work on healing your inner child.

Learning to connect with the Spirit World is part of who we are. Developing the skill and confidence takes time, persistence, and practice. Learning the language of Spirit, recognizing signs and messages, does not happen overnight.

One thing that is so awesome is that the Spirit World's love and support is with you your entire lifetime. As you heal and gain the strength to move forward after a passing or other major life changes, you'll still have access to heightened intuition, Divine guidance, and support when making life changes and the wisdom to solve everyday problems with ease.

Inviting the Spirit World into your life is a daily practice. You are not a burden to those in the Spirit World who want to support you and help you lead a happy life. Learning to make your life work is part of your mission in life. The Spirit World cannot do it for us, but they will help us along the way.

Depending on where you are in your life, your Spirit Team will show up to support you in different ways and in different times. I ask for help when I need wisdom to solve an issue. I ask for Divine guidance regularly to make sure I'm on the right path or when I need a *"next step."* I talk to my loved ones and let them know I love them often and ask for them to let me know they are with me. When I am scared about the future, I ask for comfort and support. I've been able to heal personal relationships with people in the Spirit World that I was not able to heal on this side.

I keep a journal of all the awesome experiences so that I can be reminded of how many times they have showed up in my life. Let me share with you a few stories of how the Spirit World has shown up for me.

I mentioned earlier how my grandmother showed up unexpectedly in a healing meditation. That one experience healed a place in my heart that had been numb. Her visit, which lasted about three minutes or so, left me feeling worthy of love and with a sense of being forgiven. I didn't even know the source of my *"not feeling enough"* that had affected every part of my life was from my shame and regret for not being there for her when she passed. Thank you, Wawa! (That's what I called her.) Once again, you came to my rescue.

Becoming aware of my Higher Self gave me a new sense of aliveness and power. It gave me the courage to trust my inner nudge and leave my corporate job. I had felt the knowing that I needed to leave, but I was not sure what to do. I meditated and waited for guidance. I received the knowing that I needed to help people by doing readings. Connecting to God and my Spirit Guides on a regular basis gave me the courage to take the leap of faith and start my own psychic and mediumship reading practice. The courage and trust came AFTER I followed the guidance from my Spirit Team. In fact, I was filled with fear every night for over a month because I KNEW it was the right step forward. I couldn't unknow it.

One day this simple wisdom came to me. I can't remember if it came in meditation or while I was driving to work: I can always go back. I'm leaving on good terms. I can try it for six months at 100 percent, and if it doesn't work out, I can always go back. This simple yet profound guidance did not come while I was crying out of fear of making a mistake. It came during a quiet moment later. Now, thirteen years later, I'm so glad that guidance came. I still use it today when I'm trying something new and afraid of the outcome.

Working with my Spirit Guides has been very helpful when I feel stuck, need inspiration, or am writing new meditations and teaching. I don't know my Spirit Guides' names; however, I can recognize their presence with me in meditation. I've learned to trust Spirit World timing. Guidance does not always show up in meditation. It shows up with signs of synchrony, quiet recurring thoughts, and in moments of realization. I actually get some of my guidance while in the shower or washing dishes.

A few years back, I was feeling an inner shift and went into guided meditation.

I asked for guidance about next steps for my work. I let go of my expectation of when I would get my answer. Surprise, surprise! During that specific meditation, I was shown an image of myself working with a group of people. I was thrilled even though I did not really know how to get all that going yet. Within a few months, a friend of mine suggested the name of a person who helped create online courses. I checked the person out, signed up for a class, and have been overjoyed working with students in groups for over three years now.

For me, Jesus is one of my Spirit Guides, and I call on him to help me when I am worried about others. One profound experience happened when I was worried about my son finding a job that suited him. He is a hard worker and has a great work ethic. Supporting himself is very important to him. He is an adult so I don't offer advice unless he asks. One day, I had my son on my mind. I prayed about it and said, *"I'm calling on the King. Please help my son as he is in need."* I let it go and went about my work for the day.

The next morning, my son called and asked me to drive around with him on a job hunt. I said yes and we arranged a time to meet. We drove around and talked about his interests and such. We were at the end of our search when I was drawn to a Help Wanted sign at a place of business. I said, *"Let's stop in here and get an application."* He seemed a little nervous and a bit tired from our day's adventure, but he decided to go in. He went in to get an application, and thirty minutes later he came out with a start date. I know the Spirit World helped guide our search and mission that day.

I've felt the Spirit World's presence in all my readings. I've heard them, seen them, sensed their energy. I rely on them when sharing messages with my clients. Recognizing and trusting the signs of my loved ones has been periodic. They do come in my dreams occasionally but more often in my daily life. One reason is because the Spirit World is intelligent – they come when they know there is a need.

For the most part, I've found acceptance with loss. I still long to see my loved ones and hug them in the physical, especially my mom, but I know they are with me and will be there when I need them.

After my mom's funeral, my son and daughter-in-law and I were flying back to Tampa. We had an early flight. While we were waiting to board, I looked up at the empty chairs in front of me and saw my mom and dad smiling and waving at me. At first, I looked at my son and thought, If this is real, they'll be there when I look again. I did a double-take, and they were still there. It was comforting and exciting all at the same time. I felt tears of joy rolling down my cheek. They were together – no pain, no struggle, happy – seeing us off at the airport. That memory will stay with me until I see them in Heaven.

Sometimes a visit from a loved one is for someone else. My mom was going into the hospital for some tests. She had serious issues, and the doctor rushed everything. I was in Houston doing a class. The morning of Mom's tests, my dad showed up in my morning meditation, clear as day. I was blown away. He said, *"Tell your mom she will be okay."* I was shocked because he usually shows up in other ways in my waking day and a few times in my dreams. I called her right away. She was waiting to go in for her tests. I told her about Dad's visit in my meditation and told her his message. She was excited to hear from him too. I told her what he said and told her to have faith, that she would be okay no matter what the test results showed. She went through treatment and made a full recovery. The cancer never returned. She lived several more years. When she would get afraid or worried, I would remind her that Daddy said she would be okay. I trusted he visited exactly when we all needed hope the most.

Let's be all that we are created to be. Let's shine our light and love into this world to make it a better place. Some people say life is easy. That has not been the case for me. Some days it feels like a rocky road, and I don't have any shoes on. Some days I'm flying in the clouds, but it has not been all rainbows and unicorns for me. The reason I feel called to serve you and others is because of the pain that I have struggled with and that I have overcome – and you have the same empowerment.

If you are drawn to this work, then you've experienced some kind of pain or struggle in your life and something in you says it's time to rise up and be all that you can be. Maybe that new purpose is self-love, letting go, and not being afraid to move forward and try new things. Maybe it's learning how to connect and communicate with your loved ones, knowing your loved ones are with you, learning how to manage your money, learning how to do readings, building your business, giving up workaholism, or healing relationships. Whatever it is, let's make a commitment together to work on it.

I honor you and support you in your healing path, and I want to see you shine. I believe in YOU. Connecting to the Spirit World will open a whole new chapter of growth and living beyond your expectations. I encourage you to go back and review the five strategies once a month and see where you are in your healing process. It's my heart-felt mission to help guide you and support you to be all that God created you to be – which is love and energy and purpose. Know that just you being alive, you're giving something to this world.

You have taken a big step in your healing process. I hope you will continue your healing journey. There is love, healing, support, wisdom, and guidance waiting for you.

Working through the five strategies is an awesome beginning. I'm also going to share with you an overview of my signature 7-Step Process for Connecting to the Spirit World. I've been teaching this process to students several years now and am thrilled to share this with you. This process of seven stages works for anyone who wants to grow spiritually with the Spirit World.

7 STEPS TO SPIRITUAL GROWTH

AWAKENING You are already in this stage because are reading this guidebook. This is the stage where we become aware of things outside our normal perceptions and senses. You may have an inner knowing. You may sense things and have vivid dreams or remember past lives. This may happen naturally or you may have a catalyst experience like the passing of a loved one, a change in health, or the feeling of an inner calling that initiates a search for greater understanding, knowledge, and wisdom. Experiences in this stage may be subtle or they may be profound.

AWARENESS Once we have that awakening, whether it was gradual or sudden, we can begin to develop awareness that we are spiritual beings, awareness of our natural extrasensory gifts and qualities, and awareness of all that is outside of normal everyday experiences. Awareness is the stage where you begin to know your Higher Self and explore the energy that you are giving and receiving. Two keys to this stage are recognizing your Higher Self and developing the ability to focus and stay in the present moment. Most people struggle with recognizing signs and trusting their intuition because they skip this vital step.

ALIGNMENT is the stage where we begin to mentally and telepathically set an intention to connect with those in spirit and build rapport with our Spirit Guides, loved ones, Angels, and God. We consciously align with them. We start to partner with our Spirit Team and we also begin to open up to our loved ones in Spirit. We begin to partner with the invisible world.

ACTIVATING is where we explore our chakra system and consciously turn on our extrasensory senses for intuition and connection. Doing this strengthens contact with Spirit Guides, Angels, loved ones, and the ability to access Divine guidance. We intentionally activate our chakras, our energy, our physical senses, and our extrasensory senses and begin applying those in our life at a higher level. We look for those moments in our life when we can ask for guidance or connect with a loved one in Spirit. We activate our intuitive senses and being, applying them to our daily life both to connect with our Higher Self and our loved ones as well as to gain answers about questions we may have in life.

APPLYING is the stage where we learn to manifest by getting out of our own way, asking for guidance as we move forward and watching for signs as we go. It's like following the breadcrumbs in the fairytale Hansel and Gretel. I got my initial message, and now I'm going to follow the breadcrumbs – the signs. This is the stage where we begin to apply all that we've learned and we also notice the results of our spiritual growth in our life. The applying stage is going to be a lifelong building of trust. You'll have moments where you completely trust, as if you have taken a leap of faith.

ALLOWING is the emotional phase where we begin to recognize lower energy and emotions in our life: depression, grief, sadness, fear, worry. We begin to notice how we feel, and then we begin to consciously allow higher feelings of enlightenment, joy, courage, willingness, and resonance to come forward. This is also how we build our confidence, by noticing and acknowledging the intuitive feelings and messages that we receive. Allowing is choosing the positive feelings and experiences and letting go of lower energies and emotions that may hold us back.

ATTUNEMENT is the stage where we are consciously observing our energy, tuning into our Higher Self and living our authentic life. We may feel moments of deep blissfulness. We feel a deeper connection to the Universe. We are in balance, mind, body and soul. We have a clear knowing that the Spirit World will manifest and support us in our decisions. Attunement is about mastering positive spiritual habits such as merging mind with Spirit on a regular basis.

To learn more about my 7-Step workshops and classes, visit **www.jenniferfarmer.com**

I'd like to leave you with three important truths for your journey:

- Love never dies.
- You don't have to be a medium to connect to your loved ones.
- Spirit World offers profound love and support to all.

The exercises and meditations for this section are ready and waiting for you. The Spirit World is ready and waiting to support you on your healing journey.

I welcome your feedback and suggestions. I would love to know what strategies you like and how they came to life for you.

Contact: **info@jenniferfarmer.com**

EXERCISE 9

CONNECT TO THE SPIRIT WORLD

MAKE THE CONNECTION - BUILD YOUR RAPPORT

Connecting to the Spirit World takes time and attention. The most important part of improving your connection and rapport with your Spirit Team is communication. You can choose to just talk to them in your mind or heart or out loud. They are with you and hear you. You are always connected Spirit to Spirit.

Writing letters can bring the Spirit World to life in a new way. This can strengthen the bond between our two worlds. I write letters when I need to feel a closer connection. Writing my thoughts, feelings and experiences down makes it real for me. Here are just a few ways that I use letters to talk to my Spirit Team.

- For me, I write letters to God on a regular basis. It keeps my focus and attention on my Higher Purpose and builds trust. I include five things I am grateful for in my life and personal requests and prayers for myself and others.
- When I am going through a tough time with missing my loved ones, I will write them a letter. I am honest about my regrets, anger, and conflicts with them. I also include why I am grateful for them in my life.
- When I am doing healing work with others, I read a prayer I wrote to God and my Spirit Guides to raise my mind and heart to the Higher Good. It also reminds me I'm not alone.

Experiment with writing a letter to members on your Spirit Team. Write a letter to them. You can write to God, Angels, Spirit Guides and your loved ones. Tell them how you are handling things and what is going on with you. Don't hold anything back. Be honest. Share your regrets, fears, frustrations and things you have on your mind and heart. You can ask for help making your connection stronger. Let them know you love them and miss them. Let them know you are doing the best you can at living life to the fullest. Don't forget to ask them for help and signs along the way. They will be with you.

EXAMPLE 1:

Dear God,

Thank you for the blessings in my life. Thank you for guiding me to the right doctor for my headaches. I'm hopeful. Thank you for my friends. Thank you for giving me the courage to face my fears and the strength to keep going. Thank you for helping me with making all my bills this month and for the home I live in now.

I pray that I am a blessing to everyone I talk to and share with today. I pray that others will be helped by my actions, words and deeds. Please impress your love and will upon my mind and heart so I can be all that you created me to be.

Love,
Jennifer

EXAMPLE 2:

Dear Mom,

I miss you. Mother's Day is coming up. I'm trying not to be sad. I am already thinking ahead and planning a day with James and Katee. I hope you will watch over us. We love and miss you. It is good you are in Heaven now. I would be out of my mind with worry right now with all that is going on in the nursing homes. I've been sensing you around me lately. I know you love me and am grateful you are with me. We've been through a lot together. I forgive you for all the mean and hurtful things you said to me while you were here...Every last one of them. I know you were just afraid for me and mad at me. In my heart I know you did the very best you could. Thank you for loving me even when I was hard to deal with. I love you forever.

Love, Jen
P.S. Tell daddy I said hello and that I love him too.

WORKSHEET 14

Dear: _____

WORKSHEET 14

Dear: _____

WORKSHEET 14

Dear: _____

EXERCISE 10

MAKE THE CONNECTION WITH MEDITATION

MEDITATIONS:

Meditation raises your mind and energy to a higher frequency. It helps build a bridge of connection between our two worlds. With practice, you'll feel lighter. You'll increase your senses so you can recognize visits and signs from the Spirit World.

Enter your meditations without expectations. Keeping this attitude will prove to be the most beneficial for you throughout your learning process and journey. Each practice will provide a unique experience. No two practice sessions are the same. Finally, please do not use any of these meditations while driving a car, operating machinery, or doing anything that requires your complete concentration.

Pick one of the following meditations. I recommend starting with the *Clear Your Mind* meditation first. Set a goal to practice for seven days in a row. Then choose another meditation and set a goal to practice seven days in a row. Then choose the final meditation and set a goal to practice seven days in a row. This will give you a 21-day meditation foundation. I have included a 21-day journal to help you keep track of your experiences and progress.

Less than perfect is OK. If you miss a day or two, no need to start over. Just keep going.

There are three meditations in this section to choose from:
1) *Clear Your Mind Meditation*
2) *Mindfulness Meditation*
3) *Healing Grief Meditation*

Request access to your **FREE** bonus MP3 downloads for this exercise by visiting
https://jenniferfarmer.com/bookbonus/

MEDITATION JOURNAL

MEDITATION EXPERIENCE JOURNAL

EXAMPLE:

☒ **DAY 1:** <u>Clear Your Mind Meditation</u>   ☒ Guided   ☐ Silence   ☐ Other

Date: <u>Monday, May 1, 2020</u>   How long: <u>10 minutes</u>

How well were you able to relax your body?
☒ Not so great   ☐ Making progress   ☐ Getting better and better

How well were you able to focus on the breath or following the guided practice?
☐ Not so great   ☒ Making progress   ☐ Getting better and better

Were you able to let go of the outside world or come back to the meditation when thoughts came up?
☒ Not so great   ☐ Making progress   ☐ Getting better and better

My Notes: <u>It took me a little longer to relax. I forgot to turn the phone off and had to start over. I felt some tingling on the top of my head and I saw blue and yellow swirls.</u>

MEDITATION JOURNAL

☐ **DAY 1:** _____ ☐ Guided   ☐ Silence   ☐ Other

Date: _____ How long: _____

How well were you able to relax your body?
☐ Not so great   ☐ Making progress   ☐ Getting better and better

How well were you able to focus on the breath or following the guided practice?
☐ Not so great   ☐ Making progress   ☐ Getting better and better

Were you able to let go of the outside world or come back to the meditation when thoughts came up?
☐ Not so great   ☐ Making progress   ☐ Getting better and better

My Notes: _____

_____

_____

☐ **DAY 2:** _____ ☐ Guided   ☐ Silence   ☐ Other

Date: _____ How long: _____

How well were you able to relax your body?
☐ Not so great   ☐ Making progress   ☐ Getting better and better

How well were you able to focus on the breath or following the guided practice?
☐ Not so great   ☐ Making progress   ☐ Getting better and better

Were you able to let go of the outside world or come back to the meditation when thoughts came up?
☐ Not so great   ☐ Making progress   ☐ Getting better and better

My Notes: _____

_____

_____

MEDITATION JOURNAL

☐ **DAY 3:** _____ ☐ Guided ☐ Silence ☐ Other

Date: _____ How long: _____

How well were you able to relax your body?
☐ Not so great ☐ Making progress ☐ Getting better and better

How well were you able to focus on the breath or following the guided practice?
☐ Not so great ☐ Making progress ☐ Getting better and better

Were you able to let go of the outside world or come back to the meditation when thoughts came up?
☐ Not so great ☐ Making progress ☐ Getting better and better

My Notes: _____

_____

_____

☐ **DAY 4:** _____ ☐ Guided ☐ Silence ☐ Other

Date: _____ How long: _____

How well were you able to relax your body?
☐ Not so great ☐ Making progress ☐ Getting better and better

How well were you able to focus on the breath or following the guided practice?
☐ Not so great ☐ Making progress ☐ Getting better and better

Were you able to let go of the outside world or come back to the meditation when thoughts came up?
☐ Not so great ☐ Making progress ☐ Getting better and better

My Notes: _____

_____

MEDITATION JOURNAL

☐ **DAY 5:** _____ ☐ Guided ☐ Silence ☐ Other

Date: _____ How long: _____

How well were you able to relax your body?
☐ Not so great   ☐ Making progress   ☐ Getting better and better

How well were you able to focus on the breath or following the guided practice?
☐ Not so great   ☐ Making progress   ☐ Getting better and better

Were you able to let go of the outside world or come back to the meditation when thoughts came up?
☐ Not so great   ☐ Making progress   ☐ Getting better and better

My Notes: _____
_____
_____

☐ **DAY 6:** _____ ☐ Guided ☐ Silence ☐ Other

Date: _____ How long: _____

How well were you able to relax your body?
☐ Not so great   ☐ Making progress   ☐ Getting better and better

How well were you able to focus on the breath or following the guided practice?
☐ Not so great   ☐ Making progress   ☐ Getting better and better

Were you able to let go of the outside world or come back to the meditation when thoughts came up?
☐ Not so great   ☐ Making progress   ☐ Getting better and better

My Notes: _____
_____
_____

MEDITATION JOURNAL

☐ **DAY 7:** _____ ☐ Guided ☐ Silence ☐ Other

Date:_____ How long:_____

How well were you able to relax your body?
☐ Not so great ☐ Making progress ☐ Getting better and better

How well were you able to focus on the breath or following the guided practice?
☐ Not so great ☐ Making progress ☐ Getting better and better

Were you able to let go of the outside world or come back to the meditation when thoughts came up?
☐ Not so great ☐ Making progress ☐ Getting better and better

My Notes: _____

_____

_____

☐ **DAY 8:** _____ ☐ Guided ☐ Silence ☐ Other

Date:_____ How long:_____

How well were you able to relax your body?
☐ Not so great ☐ Making progress ☐ Getting better and better

How well were you able to focus on the breath or following the guided practice?
☐ Not so great ☐ Making progress ☐ Getting better and better

Were you able to let go of the outside world or come back to the meditation when thoughts came up?
☐ Not so great ☐ Making progress ☐ Getting better and better

My Notes: _____

_____

_____

MEDITATION JOURNAL

☐ **DAY 9:** _____ ☐ Guided ☐ Silence ☐ Other

Date: _____ How long: _____

How well were you able to relax your body?
☐ Not so great ☐ Making progress ☐ Getting better and better

How well were you able to focus on the breath or following the guided practice?
☐ Not so great ☐ Making progress ☐ Getting better and better

Were you able to let go of the outside world or come back to the meditation when thoughts came up?
☐ Not so great ☐ Making progress ☐ Getting better and better

My Notes: _____
_____
_____

☐ **DAY 10:** _____ ☐ Guided ☐ Silence ☐ Other

Date: _____ How long: _____

How well were you able to relax your body?
☐ Not so great ☐ Making progress ☐ Getting better and better

How well were you able to focus on the breath or following the guided practice?
☐ Not so great ☐ Making progress ☐ Getting better and better

Were you able to let go of the outside world or come back to the meditation when thoughts came up?
☐ Not so great ☐ Making progress ☐ Getting better and better

My Notes: _____
_____
_____

MEDITATION JOURNAL

☐ **DAY 11:** _____ ☐ Guided ☐ Silence ☐ Other

Date: _____ How long: _____

How well were you able to relax your body?
☐ Not so great   ☐ Making progress   ☐ Getting better and better

How well were you able to focus on the breath or following the guided practice?
☐ Not so great   ☐ Making progress   ☐ Getting better and better

Were you able to let go of the outside world or come back to the meditation when thoughts came up?
☐ Not so great   ☐ Making progress   ☐ Getting better and better

My Notes: _____

_____

_____

☐ **DAY 12:** _____ ☐ Guided ☐ Silence ☐ Other

Date: _____ How long: _____

How well were you able to relax your body?
☐ Not so great   ☐ Making progress   ☐ Getting better and better

How well were you able to focus on the breath or following the guided practice?
☐ Not so great   ☐ Making progress   ☐ Getting better and better

Were you able to let go of the outside world or come back to the meditation when thoughts came up?
☐ Not so great   ☐ Making progress   ☐ Getting better and better

My Notes: _____

_____

_____

MEDITATION JOURNAL

☐ DAY 13: _____ ☐ Guided   ☐ Silence   ☐ Other
Date: _____ How long: _____

How well were you able to relax your body?
☐ Not so great   ☐ Making progress   ☐ Getting better and better

How well were you able to focus on the breath or following the guided practice?
☐ Not so great   ☐ Making progress   ☐ Getting better and better

Were you able to let go of the outside world or come back to the meditation when thoughts came up?
☐ Not so great   ☐ Making progress   ☐ Getting better and better

My Notes: _____
_____
_____

☐ DAY 14: _____ ☐ Guided   ☐ Silence   ☐ Other
Date: _____ How long: _____

How well were you able to relax your body?
☐ Not so great   ☐ Making progress   ☐ Getting better and better

How well were you able to focus on the breath or following the guided practice?
☐ Not so great   ☐ Making progress   ☐ Getting better and better

Were you able to let go of the outside world or come back to the meditation when thoughts came up?
☐ Not so great   ☐ Making progress   ☐ Getting better and better

My Notes: _____
_____
_____

MEDITATION JOURNAL

☐ **DAY 15:** _____ ☐ Guided ☐ Silence ☐ Other

Date: _____ How long: _____

How well were you able to relax your body?
☐ Not so great ☐ Making progress ☐ Getting better and better

How well were you able to focus on the breath or following the guided practice?
☐ Not so great ☐ Making progress ☐ Getting better and better

Were you able to let go of the outside world or come back to the meditation when thoughts came up?
☐ Not so great ☐ Making progress ☐ Getting better and better

My Notes: _____
_____
_____

☐ **DAY 16:** _____ ☐ Guided ☐ Silence ☐ Other

Date: _____ How long: _____

How well were you able to relax your body?
☐ Not so great ☐ Making progress ☐ Getting better and better

How well were you able to focus on the breath or following the guided practice?
☐ Not so great ☐ Making progress ☐ Getting better and better

Were you able to let go of the outside world or come back to the meditation when thoughts came up?
☐ Not so great ☐ Making progress ☐ Getting better and better

My Notes: _____
_____
_____

MEDITATION JOURNAL

☐ DAY 17: _____ ☐ Guided ☐ Silence ☐ Other
Date: _____ How long: _____

How well were you able to relax your body?
☐ Not so great   ☐ Making progress   ☐ Getting better and better

How well were you able to focus on the breath or following the guided practice?
☐ Not so great   ☐ Making progress   ☐ Getting better and better

Were you able to let go of the outside world or come back to the meditation when thoughts came up?
☐ Not so great   ☐ Making progress   ☐ Getting better and better

My Notes: _____
_____
_____

☐ DAY 18: _____ ☐ Guided ☐ Silence ☐ Other
Date: _____ How long: _____

How well were you able to relax your body?
☐ Not so great   ☐ Making progress   ☐ Getting better and better

How well were you able to focus on the breath or following the guided practice?
☐ Not so great   ☐ Making progress   ☐ Getting better and better

Were you able to let go of the outside world or come back to the meditation when thoughts came up?
☐ Not so great   ☐ Making progress   ☐ Getting better and better

My Notes: _____
_____
_____

MEDITATION JOURNAL

☐ **DAY 19:** _____ ☐ Guided ☐ Silence ☐ Other

Date: _____ How long: _____

How well were you able to relax your body?
☐ Not so great   ☐ Making progress   ☐ Getting better and better

How well were you able to focus on the breath or following the guided practice?
☐ Not so great   ☐ Making progress   ☐ Getting better and better

Were you able to let go of the outside world or come back to the meditation when thoughts came up?
☐ Not so great   ☐ Making progress   ☐ Getting better and better

My Notes: _____
_____
_____

☐ **DAY 20:** _____ ☐ Guided ☐ Silence ☐ Other

Date: _____ How long: _____

How well were you able to relax your body?
☐ Not so great   ☐ Making progress   ☐ Getting better and better

How well were you able to focus on the breath or following the guided practice?
☐ Not so great   ☐ Making progress   ☐ Getting better and better

Were you able to let go of the outside world or come back to the meditation when thoughts came up?
☐ Not so great   ☐ Making progress   ☐ Getting better and better

My Notes: _____
_____
_____

MEDITATION JOURNAL

☐ DAY 21: _____ ☐ Guided ☐ Silence ☐ Other

Date: _____ How long: _____

How well were you able to relax your body?
☐ Not so great   ☐ Making progress   ☐ Getting better and better

How well were you able to focus on the breath or following the guided practice?
☐ Not so great   ☐ Making progress   ☐ Getting better and better

Were you able to let go of the outside world or come back to the meditation when thoughts came up?
☐ Not so great   ☐ Making progress   ☐ Getting better and better

My Notes: _____

_____

_____

FINAL REFLECTIONS: _____

_____

_____

_____

_____

_____

_____

_____

_____

_____

_____

MEDITATION 1

CLEAR YOUR MIND MEDITATION

With the purchase of this book, you receive free access to an online learning library as an added bonus. To get access to the learning library and the MP3 download for this meditation, send your request for your free bonus.
https://jenniferfarmer.com/bookbonus/

Log in to your learning library to download the MP3 guided meditation.
https://jennifer-farmer.mykajabi.com/library

Instructions for following written practice:
- Follow the practice with your eyes open.
- Spend a couple of moments for each instruction.
- In some sections, I'll ask you to close your eyes for a few moments.
- If you like you can close your eyes anywhere you like in order to allow the intention of the meditation to settle in your mind.

Let's begin:
Learning to clear your mind is the first step toward clarity. This meditation can be used any time you need to clear your mind or raise your level of awareness and consciousness. So, let's begin now by getting comfortable.

Choose a quiet place, free from distractions and disturbances.
Sit or lie down. Make sure your back is well supported.
Now take a nice deep breath in and exhale out.
Another deep breath in and exhale out. Very good.
Settle more into this space where you are. Nice and easy.

Close your eyes for a moment and notice the natural rhythm of your breath as you breathe in and out.

MEDITATION 1

Relax your body a little more.

Let all the muscles in your body release.
Excellent.
Feel the rise and fall of your chest.
Breathe a little deeper into your lungs.
And gently exhale out.

Let the mind begin to slow down, gently bringing your focus to the words on this page.

Close your eyes for a few moments and let your mind slow down.
Breathe a little deeper into your lungs and gently exhale out.

Now, as you exhale out, release any worries or concerns that may be lingering in your mind.

Imagine as you breathe out letting go of all your worries.
Let them all go.
The breath is peaceful and cleansing.
Feel it move through your body as you breathe in and breathe out.
Relax all the muscles in your body.

Close your eyes for a moment and let go of any lingering tension.
Take a full breath in all the way down to your belly.
Gently exhale out.
The peaceful, subtle energy of the breath moves through your body filling every organ and every cell.

Close your eyes for a moment and imagine your whole body being at peace.
Nice breath in.

MEDITATION 1

The spiritual being that you are comes to life more and more with each breath.
Breathing in and breathing out.
Close your eyes and imagine your inner power, your own energy and presence emerge.

You're doing wonderful.
Breathing in and breathing out.
Enjoy the feeling of this peaceful energy as it grows stronger within you.

I want you to imagine your energy.
This subtle energy you've been feeling is a light.
You can make the light any color that feels good to you.
Close your eyes for a moment and feel the presence of a light.

Adjust your inner light to make it as bright as you want it to be.
Make it clear, warm, and powerful. It's your inner light.

Close your eyes a moment and imagine your inner light radiating through your whole being bright and clear for the next few minutes on your own.

You are doing it, let your inner light expand more and more with each breath.
Take another big breath in and exhale out. Very good.

Take a minute more, close your eyes and feel your inner power, your own energy and presence.
Nice and easy. Big breath in. Bring your awareness back to where you're sitting or lying down.
Come back more and more.
Gently move your fingers and toes.
Take a nice big stretch.
Another full breath in. Very good.

Congratulations on completing this meditation practice.

MEDITATION 2

STILLNESS, AWARENESS MEDITATION

HERE'S HOW TO GET STARTED:

1. Find a quiet time and space where you won't be disturbed.
2. Sit or lie comfortably. You may even want to invest in a cushion or meditation chair.
3. Close your eyes.
4. Breathe in and out naturally.
5. Focus all your attention on the breath and on how the body moves with each inhalation and exhalation.
6. Notice the rise and fall of your chest as you breathe. Be aware of the breath and follow it as it travels through your body. Bring your attention to your lungs, chest, shoulders, ribs, and tummy and how they are moving in and out with each breath.
7. As you are breathing in, consciously let go of tension in your body. Imagine your body relaxing.
8. As you breathe out, let your muscles relax. Take a minute and feel this relaxation in your entire body. Practice relaxing your shoulders, your arms, your hips, your legs, and your toes.
9. Simply focus your attention on your breath without controlling pace or intensity. If your mind wanders, return your focus back to your breath.
10. Practice this for five to ten minutes at a time.

MEDITATION 3

HEALING GRIEF WITH THE SPIRIT WORLD MEDITATION

For your **FREE** bonus access to the learning library or help logging in:
https://jenniferfarmer.com/bookbonus/

Log in to your learning library to download the MP3 guided meditation.
https://jennifer-farmer.mykajabi.com/library

If you are ready, we're going to take all the painful emotions we have – grief, loss, regret, anger, fear, shame – and we're going to give it all up to the Spirit World. We're taking it to the Spirit World in a guided meditation and beginning our healing transformation with the help of the Spirit World.

Instructions for following written practice:
- Follow the practice with your eyes open.
- Spend a couple of moments for each instruction.
- In some sections, I'll ask you to close your eyes for a few moments.
- If you like you can close your eyes anywhere you like in order to allow the intention of the meditation to settle in your mind.
- Make sure you won't be disturbed for the next 15-20 minutes.

Let's begin:
Take a nice deep breath in and easily exhale out.
Another deep breath in and gently exhale out. Let yourself relax on the exhale.
Take another deep breath in and exhale out easily and naturally.
Begin to settle more where you are. It's safe to rest your mind and body.

Relax your body and settle into the space you are in. Just breathing in and gently exhaling out.

MEDITATION 3

Begin to notice the natural rhythm of your breath as you breathe in and out.

Feel the rise and fall of your chest.
Breathe a little deeper into your lungs. And gently exhale out.
Settle down a little more.
Another deep breath in and gently exhale out.
Let go of any lingering tension in your mind or body.
Just breathing in and exhaling out.
Get more comfortable being still and calm. Gently breathe in and exhale out.

Now close your eyes for a moment and imagine standing in front of a bridge.
Visualize the bridge as a rainbow of light.
The rainbow offers safe passage between our two worlds.

Nice breath in and easily exhale out.
It is your pathway to healing and peace.
You're safe and ready to take this journey.

Keep in mind the picture of a rainbow. Close your eyes a moment and visualize a beautiful rainbow and the lights from the rainbow coming toward you.

Imagine now standing at the foot of the rainbow.

Nice breath in here. Let yourself begin to easily climb up the arc of the rainbow. See and feel yourself moving upward.

The amazing rainbow of light extends upward farther than what your eyes can see. With each step you take, the rainbow is taking you higher and higher.

Let yourself become one with the rainbow moving upward. Allow the healing energy of the rainbow to wash away your feelings of grief and pain.

MEDITATION 3

Nice breath in and easily exhale out.

Releasing your feelings of grief as your grief bubbles up within you.

That's right, let your feelings, your pains and struggles, bubble up to the surface.
It's safe to pull them up because we're going to release them.

Imagine letting go of the feelings.
Close your eyes and imagine letting go and watching them
fade away into the healing energy of the rainbow.

Nice breath in here. And easily exhale out.
You are becoming lighter and lighter with each breath in.

Imagine now moving forward even higher in the rainbow.

Allow yourself to be one with the colors of the rainbow.

Nice breath in here. And easily exhale out.

You're transcending into the spiritual realm.
It's a wonderful dream atmosphere.

Close your eyes here and imagine being in a realm of peace and healing.
Open yourself up to it. Release your feelings of sadness, loss, and emptiness.

Visualize them disappearing through the colors of the rainbow.

Allow yourself to be at peace in this moment.
Nice breath in here and easily exhale out following along with me.

MEDITATION 3

Another breath in here.
Now I want you to visualize your heart full of love. Feel the love in you expand.

Close your eyes and visualize beautiful light coming from your heart.

Rest for a few moments and enjoy being in this healing space.
Nice breath in here.
You are doing wonderful.
Visualize yourself standing on top of the rainbow.
Imagine that the rainbow of light is bringing you the energy of peace.
The feeling of peace is washing through you.

Close your eyes for a few moments and be at peace in the rainbow of light.
Stay here as long as you like.

Nice breath in here.
Very easily begin to move your awareness back into the room where you are.
Nice, gentle breath in and easily exhale out.
Come back more and more.
Another full breath in and easily exhale out.
Gently move your fingers and toes.
Take a nice big stretch.

Practice as often as you like. In time, you will develop your own unique way to practice. You will get better and better with each practice. Practice will promote inner peace.

NEXT STEPS

CONGRATULATIONS ON COMPLETING THIS JOURNEY!

Congratulations.

You've given yourself a wonderful gift during a very stressful time in your life. You are in a new chapter of living. I recommend going back through the exercises in a month or so and check your progress.

To learn more about the Spirit World, watch my FREE **two-part video series!**

Learning to connect with the Spirit World is part of who we are. I created a FREE two-part video series that goes into this topic in more depth. In the series we cover how to get started with connecting to the Spirit World and what to expect. It will help you begin with meditation and provide exercises for recognizing your Higher Self.

Free access is here: **https://jennifer-farmer.mykajabi.com/freeworkshop.**

Also, to learn more about my signature **7 Steps to Spiritual Growth** workshops, classes and membership, visit **www.jenniferfarmer.com.**

Please share your progress, challenges and wins with me. Leave your comments in the learning library, email me directly or share your journey on my Facebook page. Sharing will empower you and will help others connect and move forward too. **https://www.facebook.com/JenniferFarmerLLC**

NEXT STEPS

Thank you for allowing me to help you move forward in your healing journey. Your light is shining brighter.

I would love to hear from you. Please email **info@jenniferfarmer.com** with any comments, questions or if you need help accessing your online learning library.

With love and gratitude,
Jennifer

ABOUT THE AUTHOR

Jennifer Farmer is a recognized leader in her field as a gifted intuitive, medium, and spiritual teacher. Her passion is to inspire people to tap into and use the power of Spirit and intuition in their daily lives. People from all over the world and all walks of life seek out Jennifer for professional and personal development. She has created signature classes on developing intuition, spiritual growth, living your higher purpose, and healing with the Spirit World.

She accesses her intuitive strengths to help clients and students heal and move forward in their personal and professional life. For more than twelve years, she has mentored students online and around the globe in developing intuition and psychic/mediumship discovery.

She has created meditation audio recordings for personal health, improving intuition, and connecting with the Spirit World. Her healing meditations were featured in Yoga Magazine in 2010. She is the founder of the Solutions of Spirit group and the Spiritual Growth Mentoring online community for spiritual seekers and is based in North Richland Hills, Texas.

Made in United States
North Haven, CT
22 January 2022